"More than ever, we need
students in conversations t
perspectives and worldviews. Kay and Orr are those educators,
and with this book, they have gifted the field with their
insights and knowledge."

—Dr. Val Brown
Educator and founder of #ClearTheAir

"Couldn't put it down! Nineteen years as an elementary
educator and there hasn't been a year where inquiries around
race did not arise. This book is a guide to support how we
prepare our students at the youngest ages to lovingly negotiate
race in the classroom."

—Lynsey Burkins
Elementary educator

"With *We're Gonna Keep on Talking,* Matt Kay and Jennifer
Orr equip elementary teachers with something we've been
in search of for a long time: the tools and know-how to engage
our young students in meaningful conversations about race
in our classrooms. This is a book I will turn to again and again
to inform my practice. More importantly, it will give all of
us the opportunity to grapple with the type of thinking and
discussions that will ultimately lead us all, students and
teachers alike, to co-create a more just world. Thank you,
Matt and Jennifer!"

—Christina Nosek
Co-author of *To Know and Nurture a Reader*

"Jen and Matt show us what is possible when educators listen to children, are brave, and actively engage in the difficult conversations that our youngest children are already having about race, identity, and social issues. It is our responsibility as educators to have meaningful race conversations with our youngest learners and guide them into these difficult conversations, not as isolated lessons, but as a way of being and living in our classroom communities. *We're Gonna Keep on Talking* shows us how we can trust the children and ourselves to have race conversations, why they are so critical, and is full of honest and relatable stories about having these conversations in our classrooms. This book has a sense of urgency running through it and will support you as you go into your classroom and "keep on talking" with your children. We cannot step back from these conversations as there is not a minute to waste. Our children, our communities, and our world deserve spaces where meaningful race conversations are encouraged, supported, and celebrated. This book will be the one you carry with you in your school bag, refer to often, and take Matt and Jen with you into your classroom as you have these courageous and essential conversations with learners from Pre-K to upper elementary."

—Katie Keier
PreK teacher and co-author of
*Catching Readers Before They Fall:
Supporting Readers Who Struggle, K-4*

WE'RE GONNA KEEP ON TALKING

WE'RE GONNA KEEP ON TALKING

HOW TO LEAD MEANINGFUL RACE CONVERSATIONS IN THE ELEMENTARY CLASSROOM

MATTHEW R. KAY
JENNIFER ORR

Routledge
Taylor & Francis Group

NEW YORK AND LONDON

A Stenhouse Book

First published 2023 by Stenhouse Publishers

Published 2024 by Routledge
605 Third Avenue, New York, NY 10017
4 Park Square, Milton Park, Abingdon, Oxon OX14 4RN

*Routledge is an imprint of the Taylor & Francis Group,
an informa business*

Introduction, "Ain't Gonna Let Nobody Turn Me Around" lyrics.
    © Source Unknown.
Figure I.1, © Getty Images.
Figure I.2, © Evelyn Hockstein. Used by permission of Reuters Pictures.
Figure I.3, © Bob Adelman.
Figure 1.3, *Rez Dogs* by Joseph Bruchac. © 2022 Joseph Bruchac.
    Used by permission of Penguin Random House.
Figure 5.2, © Architect of the Capitol.
Figures 6.3a–6.3e, Voter Turnout Demographics by the Elect Project.
    © Michael McDonald. Electproject.org.

Library of Congress Cataloging-in-Publication Data

Names: Kay, Matthew R., 1983– author. | Orr, Jennifer, author.
Title: We're gonna keep on talking : how to lead meaningful race
   conversations in the elementary classroom / Matthew R. Kay and Jennifer
   Orr.
Other titles: We are going to keep on talking
Description: Portsmouth, New Hampshire : Stenhouse Publishers, [2023] |
   Includes bibliographical references and index. |
Identifiers: LCCN 2022058438 | ISBN 9781625315755 (paperback)
Subjects: LCSH: Multicultural education—Study and teaching
   (Elementary)—United States. | United States—Race relations—Study and
   teaching (Elementary) | Race awareness—Study and teaching
   (Elementary)—United States. | Racism—Study and teaching
   (Elementary)—United States. | Group work in education—United States. |
   Discussion. | Elementary school teachers—In-service training—United
   States. | BISAC: EDUCATION / Professional Development | EDUCATION /
   Philosophy, Theory & Social Aspects
Classification: LCC LC1099.3 .K394 2023
   DDC 370.1170973—dc23/eng/20230322
LC record available at https://lccn.loc.gov/2022058438

Cover and interior design by Jill Shaffer
Typesetting by Eclipse Publishing Services

ISBN 13: 978-1-62531-575-5 (pbk)
ISBN 13: 978-1-03-268305-8 (ebk)

DOI: 10.4324/9781032683058

To Jeff, Kate, and Charlie, who seem to believe
I can do anything and help me believe the same.
—JEN

In loving memory of Sherrill Jones Kay, my mother,
a thirty-six-year teaching veteran
and the reason I do what I do.
"I've decided to keep you."
—MATT

CONTENTS

ACKNOWLEDGMENTS

From Jen

JO For the modeling of what it means to be a kind and thoughtful human being, I will be eternally grateful to every generation of my family, from my great-grandparents to my own children. None of us are perfect, but I have learned we can continually work to be better.

As an educator, I have a long list of people who have encouraged and supported me. I have been blessed with wonderful administrators and colleagues for a quarter century.

I am thankful for the opportunity to work with Bill and Kassia on this book. Their editorial thoughtfulness and gentle nudges have not only improved what you read here but have helped me develop my writing skills.

More than anything, I am indebted to Matt for the opportunity to be a part of this work. His wisdom, patience, and ability to find humor have been true gifts to me. Reading Matt's first book, *Not Light, But Fire*, made me a better teacher and person. Working with Matt on this book has taken that growth to another level completely.

From Matt

MK I'd like to thank my wife, Cait, for continually finding ways to support and encourage me, as both a fellow teacher and a fellow author; my father, Rosamond, for the decades of mind-sharpening debate that have modeled the discourse I want for my students; and my Aunt Connie, for her unconditional love and support.

Thanks to my principal and great friend, Chris Lehmann, for all the professional opportunities that led to the writing of this book. I will always be grateful to Dan Tobin and this book's first editor, Bill Varner, for pushing me—somewhat relentlessly—to write another book, and for believing in this concept as soon as the idea emerged. I appreciate Kassia offering her patience, expertise, and steady encouragement as Jen and I took this on. We could *not* have crossed the finish line without you, Kassia!

I am so grateful to Jen for saying yes! She brought so much to this project—her wisdom and storytelling making it better than I ever could have imagined. She is the educator that all of our children deserve, and I hope both of my girls are blessed to have teachers like her.

Speaking of which, thank you again, Dia. You *remain* a perfect gift, just in time. And to Benni, my miracle girl, thank you for holding on so fiercely to us. Daddy loves you.

INTRODUCTION

WE'RE GONNA KEEP ON TALKING

Ain't gonna let nobody turn me around
Turn me around, turn me around
Ain't gonna let nobody turn me around
I'm gonna keep on a-walkin', keep on a-talkin'
Marchin' up to freedom land.

FIGURE I.1
Children singing
freedom songs
during the Children's
Crusade of 1963 in
Birmingham, Alabama

MK In the years since *Not Light, But Fire* came out, I've met many teachers during scores of trips to schools and conferences around the country. These colleagues—and new fast friends—have been generous with their praise and gentle with their criticism. They've also been quick to give encouragement, from playful "Okay, I see you!" daps in 2019 to earnest and knowing "Hang in there!" elbow bumps in 2021. There has been plenty of advice too. First it was "Make a website!" (check!), then it was "Record an audio-book!" (check!). But far and away the most common suggestion has come as a question:

How do we do this at the elementary level?

In response to this, I would laugh, pointing to the near-perfect timing of my first daughter being born right after the *Not Light* draft was submitted to Stenhouse Publishers. The thought of writing *anything* with a bawling newborn in the house gave me heart palpitations. Also, writing a book was hard! In my 2015 book proposal, I'd told my prospective editor that, with all the ideas I had ready to go, I could crank out a book in six months. It took me two years. It wasn't just the interviews, reflections, and research but also the challenge of writing as life just barreled on. I had the best (I got married!) and the worst (my mom passed away unexpectedly) days of my life while writing *Not Light*. My school packed up and moved to a new location while I was writing *Not Light*. I juggled coaching basketball, teaching kids English and drama, and running a nonprofit slam poetry league while writing *Not Light*. I was *so* happy when writing was finished!

But more important than that, I was thoroughly intimidated by the prospect of writing for elementary teachers. My mom was one, for thirty-six years. The first time I experienced education from the teacher's side was in her classroom; the first lessons I taught were to her students. I saw and understood the incredible artistry needed to meaningfully engage our youngest students. And now, I am fully aware that my successes with secondary students are built on the foundation of elementary teachers' hard work, skill, and dedication. Even if I could find the energy and time to write for elementary colleagues, there was no way I could do it without the help of an amazing elementary teacher. When readers of *Not Light* requested an "elementary version" of the book, I would often (with tongue firmly in cheek) ask them to go in on a book with me, and we would laugh and both go on about our days.

> I saw and understood the incredible artistry needed to meaningfully engage our youngest students.

But their requests stuck with me, especially throughout the maelstrom that was 2020 and *then* the coordinated state-by-state assault on discussions of race in the classroom over the following years. Very quickly, it seemed to matter less that I was tired. What was my fatigue to a fifth-grade teacher somewhere bravely planning a powerful race conversation that was sure to upset a community? I had to try, and I was going to need an excellent elementary school teacher to coauthor such a project. Someone precisely like the author of *Demystifying Discussion*, Jennifer Orr.

JO I read *Not Light* as soon as it was published. Multiple times. I recommended it to plenty of other elementary teachers. When Matt reached out to suggest collaborating on an elementary version, I immediately said yes. Then turned to my husband and said, "I just agreed to do this . . . and I have no idea if I am able to." I've done a lot of writing in recent years. Nothing, I believe, has felt this difficult. Not long after that conversation with Matt, I read an essay by Imani Perry in which she writes, "Sometimes, I have read, people use the second person instead of 'I' when they are talking about something that is especially painful because it is less frightening if you distance yourself from it" (2021, 192). When I read it, I stopped cold. My first draft of this introduction was not written in the first person. Facing my own fears, my self-doubts as a leader of classroom race conversations, was too hard. Perry's words helped me recognize what I was doing and try again.

Having taught elementary school students for more than two decades now, I have faced and overcome many fears. Some fears (such as worrying about being younger than the parents of my students—something that is definitely not a concern these days) simply faded, thanks to aging and gaining experience, and some fears had to be faced head on. As a straight, cisgender, able-bodied, middle-class, native-English-speaking White woman, I had many fears about teaching and talking with my students about, well, just about anything. I told myself I didn't have the life experiences, the background knowledge, the expertise to talk about race, class, queerness, disability, and more.

Early in my career I didn't even have the time or energy to think too hard about race in the classroom. Everything I had went into getting to know my students, learning better how to teach and support them, and just getting through each week to crash by 8:00 p.m. on Friday. As some of the basics became ingrained and I continued learning, I began to wonder if, by not leading race conversations, I was doing my students a disservice.

Even as I pondered this question, the discomfort didn't go away. I considered whether elementary students (I taught fourth and fifth graders at this point) were too young to have these conversations. I could see plenty of people around me refusing to discuss difficult social issues with children this age, intentionally shielding them from facts some might find uncomfortable. Of course, what I wasn't seeing then was that those people, the teachers I was looking to as models, were White folks like me. When I pushed myself (and I don't like to think about how long it took me), I could see that many young children of color were *already* discussing these topics. A kindergartner who was excluded from a game at recess by her peers because of her skin color is likely to ask the adults in her life about race. A fourth grader who is relied on to be the class expert when it comes to the Civil Rights Movement or rap music will know how others see him. Children who are pushed to read, write, or research specific topics that fit stereotypes about them often question why that isn't happening to certain classmates.

4

FIGURE I.2
A parents' rights group protesting what they believe is critical race theory (CRT) being taught in schools

It took me a full decade of teaching, and three different grade levels, before I recognized that many of my young students could, and regularly did, have these conversations about race. By then, I was also a parent of two young White kids, and our interactions clarified for me how crucial race conversations were. My youngest went to two different home daycares before starting elementary school. In the first, the adults were first-generation immigrants from South Asia. In the second, the caregiver was a Black woman. My child began asking good questions about race very early on. Engaging in these conversations with a two- or three-year-old made it a lot easier for me to begin to see how to lead similar conversations with kids twice that age.

I'll admit, though, this didn't stop me from worrying about leading such conversations with my students. What if a parent got upset and complained? How should I handle colleagues who thought my students were too young for these discussions? What if, agreeing with them, my administration wouldn't support me?

Yet, in the midst of these fears, I knew what I *could* count on: my willingness to communicate openly and honestly. Because of this openness and honesty, I knew my students' families and they knew me. In my more than twenty years of teaching, I can count on one hand the number of times a family and I couldn't resolve an issue by talking together about it. My colleagues and administrators, too, were people with whom I had relationships, people with whom I've talked about teaching and the choices we make. We would work together through any reasonable question or concern, and I wouldn't allow hypothetical naysayers to stop our forward momentum.

> But the young children we spend our days with need us to keep pushing through our nervousness. To refuse to let our anxieties stifle us.

In the end, I teach young children. They are observant and they are curious. They are full of questions and frequently aware of when we, the adults in their lives, are *avoiding* certain conversations. We can tell ourselves that avoiding the topic of race is a way of remaining neutral, of not taking a stance. However, our students are aware of this avoidance, and they do not see it as neutral. They recognize the importance of their questions, and we must do the same. It is okay for us to be nervous, to be worried, and then, after trying hard, to make mistakes. But the young children we spend our days with need us to keep pushing through our nervousness. To refuse to let our anxieties stifle us. And we, as knowledgeable, thoughtful professionals, can do this work for them.

MK Before we leave this introduction, it helps to remember that these are not the first challenging times for educators determined to discuss race meaningfully in the classroom. This is not the first time that teaching the truth has been unpopular, or that authentic analysis of "controversial" topics has been legislated against. It certainly is not the first time that our youngest students' ability to tackle race issues has been underestimated by the communities that claim to believe in them the most. We teachers of good will need more than a general understanding of this history; we need to collect this history like fuel. Bad actors have tried all of this before—and they have failed because of the righteous stubbornness of teachers just like us.

I gave *Not Light, But Fire* its title to remind myself of this urgent truth-telling legacy. Frederick Douglass, in 1852, was invited to speak at Corinthian Hall by the Rochester Ladies' Anti-Slavery Society. He delivered his most famous speech that day, furiously asking the question that pops up on some of our social media feeds every Independence Day: *What to the American slave is your Fourth of July?* The withering next few paragraphs detailing the unrelenting brutality of America's antebellum slave system are brilliant, and worth every ounce of their current fame. However, for me, it's always been all about Douglass's frustration over being asked to waste his time "shedding light" on race issues, clarifying stuff for those who are disingenuously confused. A century and a half later, I can almost hear the exasperation in his voice:

Must I undertake to prove that the slave is a man? That point is conceded already. Nobody doubts it. The slaveholders themselves acknowledge it in the enactment of laws for their government . . . It is admitted in the fact that Southern statute books are covered with enactments forbidding, under severe fines and penalties, the teaching of the slave to read or to write. When you can point to any such laws, in reference to the beasts of the field, then I may consent to argue the manhood of the slave. When the dogs in your streets, when the fowls of the air, when the cattle on your hills, when the fish of the sea, and the reptiles that crawl, shall be unable to distinguish the slave from a brute, *then* will I argue with you that the slave is a man!

(*Douglass 1852*)

Douglass, an abolitionist orator whose resume attested to his boundless stamina, spoke here like a man well aware of his human limitations. While some people seemed to always have energy for

FIGURE I.3
Children carrying signs as they march in the Children's Crusade of 1963 in Birmingham, Alabama

inconsequential and showy "debates," inauthentic sermonizing, and hard-hearted trolling, he did not. He was committed to honest conversations about our nation's complex racial history, its layered racial present, and the uncertain future that was being built for all of its children. Making sure his point wasn't lost, Douglass soon bellowed, "It is not light that is needed, but fire!" (Douglass 1852). Whereas light merely illuminates injustice, fire actually does something about it.

One morning in 1963—little more than a century after Douglass described this thirst for action—scores of young Black children gathered excitedly in Birmingham, Alabama. During a series of mass meetings, they'd been told, as participant Janice Kelsey recalled years later, that "a day would come when we could really *do something* about all of these inequities we'd been experiencing" (History Channel, 2014). Inspired by these conversations, droves of students, many of them still in elementary school, had left their classes to meet at the Sixteenth Street Baptist Church. There they meant to organize themselves, and then march to nearby Kelly Ingram Park, where Jim Crow laws forbade them to play. While many of the adults in their lives had been supportive, just as many cautious parents, neighbors, and teachers had discouraged the children from attending. This reluctance made sense—and in many ways proved prescient—as the notorious Bull Connor, Birmingham's commissioner of public safety, would infamously set his dogs and fire hoses on many of the young protesters. Still, in rapidly increasing numbers, the children continued to show up. As they waited in the church, they sang freedom songs—many of which echoed Douglass's eagerness. My favorite of these, *Ain't Gonna Let Nobody Turn Me Around*, had the children proclaiming, "I'm gonna keep on a-walkin', **keep on a-talkin'** / Marchin' up to freedom land!" This, even though they were still young children. Even though they might not have had all the answers. Even though the discourse might have been scary, or unpopular, or hard. These little kids were going to keep on talking despite every obstacle that the adult world threw in their faces.

We're Gonna Keep On Talking is for teachers who share not only Frederick Douglass's hunger for authentic race discourse but also the courage of those young children who gathered in Birmingham to continue the conversation against all odds. Essentially, this is a book for teachers of young children who believe that learning to have meaningful race conversations is just as foundational as developing literacy and numeracy. For just as literacy and numeracy might enable students to better chase their dreams, a foundation in meaningful race discourse will help them to seek justice for themselves and their neighbors, to be kinder, more thoughtful, less willing to see their considerable potential hamstrung by the same old restrictive prejudices. This book is for teachers who—like us—are far from perfect, but who are willing to try to meet this moment.

> This book is for teachers who—like us—are far from perfect, but who are willing to try to meet this moment.

HOW TO USE THIS BOOK

As current classroom teachers, both of us really appreciate a good old-fashioned "plug-and-play" PD book. One that you can crack open on a stressed Monday night to find great activities for Tuesday morning. It's often efficient (or, at the very least, convenient) to find a quick resource, tool, or game that will engage your students. We love these books. We've used these books. *We're Gonna Keep On Talking*, however, is something else. While its advice will be practical, and its writing will be easy to digest, this book is not meant to be "plug-and-play." It can't be, if it is to be truthful. Success in classroom race discussions relies on too many factors for us to promise quick, all-encompassing solutions.

So how do you use this book, then? In a word, carefully. Take your time before implementing anything you read here. Ask yourself where you see your own students in Jen's stories. Ask yourself what factors matter most in your specific teaching context, and what adjustments you might need to make. If possible, read this book and do these reflections alongside like-minded colleagues, then collectively make plans that support and build upon what each of you is doing.

We are humble enough to know that seismic events might happen between our writing this book and your reading it (as Matt knows all too well, having published a book about race talk just two years before 2020). The ideas and suggestions in these pages, then, are not meant to be dogma. They are meant to be the whispered advice of two trusted veteran colleagues who, while they have not taught in *your* classroom, during *this* school year, have still "seen a few things." We're only here to share what has worked for us, and what has not.

THE ECOSYSTEM

Like living things, classroom race conversations rely on a very specific ecosystem to thrive—and on hard days, to merely survive. Without a foundation of healthy relationships, strong communication skills, and sound conversational structures, we are forced to rely on either our "sparkling" personalities or our "good luck," neither of which can be counted on to be consistent over the course of a whirlwind school year. Our goal, then, is to make our success *reliable* by making it *systemic*. To have a process that we can trust in good times and chaotic times, when our students are ready and when they are not. The chapters in Part 1 of this book will (1) show how to establish a safe space that is ready for meaningful race conversations, (2) illustrate how to improve the specific communication skills necessary to lead race discussions with young children, and (3) break down the specific pedagogical moves that lead to the best outcomes in race conversations.

CHAPTER 1

BUILDING COMMUNITY TOGETHER

There are many ways we teachers might get burned making assumptions. We might overvalue some colleague's tales of a student's misbehavior and then foolishly start off a school year trying to fuss that student into compliance—instead of seeding a quality relationship. Or we might figure that a student's neighborhood, ethnicity, or gender accurately predicts the kind of books they'd be interested in, and then only ever suggest that particular genre during independent reading time. While teaching virtually during the COVID-19 pandemic, often seeing black Zoom boxes and avatars instead of children's bright smiles, we all hopefully discovered just how dangerous it can be to assume that we know what our students are going through, how hard they are working, or what skills and knowledge they have retained. Accepting these faulty presuppositions can lead to mistakes, many of which hurt children.

But when it comes to leading race conversations in our classrooms, there is one assumption that threatens to undermine all of our hard work even before we get going. It's not one of the nefarious ones that might spring to mind, like "*These* kids can't discuss tough stuff," or "Systemic racism doesn't impact *this* population." It's assuming that the adult world *has already* offered (with our older students) or *will eventually* offer (with our youngest) an abundance of good role models for race discourse. Believing this, we might expect our older students to have already learned the best ways to earnestly engage with differing opinions about race—even though the adult world may have spent years teaching them to antagonize, troll, and gaslight. We might expect these older students to instinctively embrace complexity—even though social media might have taught them to find false comfort in absolutes. Similarly, those of us who teach our youngest students might not expect bad role models to target kids who are so very little. But they do. Our young learners see their older siblings and neighbors engaging in the discourse that has been modeled for them. They have adults in their lives—in their families and beyond—who gloss over their questions and concerns when it comes to race. And when well-meaning teachers do not properly account for bad race-talk role models (whether they be willfully poisonous or merely negligent), our attempts to discuss race might well hurt children—or set up situations where they unintentionally wound each other.

In order for us to lead meaningful race conversations with elementary-aged students, we must humbly embrace the opportunity to (often) be among the first adults to teach them *how* to discuss race issues, with both a respect for detail and a realistic understanding that such instruction will often run counter to messaging that students get from others in the adult world. This is never clearer than when we consider the specific importance of listening skills. The ability to listen well is essential for successful class-room race discourse—and yet few skills are traditionally more undervalued in American culture than listening. If kids don't know *how* to listen to each other, their verbal exchanges in class may be many things, but they will not be real conversations. Recognizing this, Matt described three listening skills in *Not Light* that he's taught and practiced with his high school students for many years. Here, we'll briefly reintroduce them, examining each one through the lens of an elementary school educator.

LISTEN PATIENTLY

When students are *listening patiently*, they are making a conscious effort to show whoever is speaking that they are paying close attention.

Anyone who has worked with elementary students for very long knows that listening patiently is not often a strength for them. Impulse control is something our young learners are still mastering, and listening patiently definitely requires them to control the impulse to jump in and share their own thoughts or questions. As an elementary teacher, Jen regularly has to remind herself that this impulse is often a good sign. Students who are having trouble listening patiently are often so excited to be a part of the conversation that they just can't wait to speak up. Something about the prompt must be good to spark this reaction! The challenge for us as teachers is to help them wait without stomping on their excitement. On her better days, when a student interrupts a classmate, Jen might say, "Hang on, Cindy, you'll get a turn to share your awesome ideas very soon. Right now we're listening to Lisa's ideas," instead of "Cindy, it's not your turn; stop interrupting." While the latter option has the potential to shut Cindy down completely, the former clearly communicates to her both that her ideas are valued and that Jen is eager to hear those ideas—while also reminding her that the class wants to hear others' ideas as well. The extra few seconds spent on this clear explanation make it less likely that Cindy will make negative assumptions about why she was not allowed to finish talking (*"Ms. Orr doesn't like me,"* or *"I'm not as smart as Lisa,"* for example). And if we explain ourselves often enough, we might even reap the benefits of our customary clarity on those occasions when we forget to be clear! Students learn that we are stopping interruptions not because they are being bad but because the student who was speaking deserves the space to finish.

We have to be thoughtful both about teaching our students how to listen patiently to their classmates and about showing them what patient listening looks and feels like. This work includes a variety of strategies:

1. Encouraging nonverbal communication such as eye contact and nodding (though without the militaristic "you will comply!" energy that we sometimes see).

2. Teaching students to first recognize and then check their instinct to interrupt or raise their hand while a classmate is talking.

3. Helping students build strategies to remember their own ideas or questions while listening to others. (More on this later.)

That's a lot to tackle, but the result of treating patient listening as a skill to be developed and reflected upon (and not just a "behavior problem") will be students who are more effective participants in classroom conversations about tough stuff. They might even take these skills into friend and family conversations.

"What does patient listening actually look (and feel) like?"

It helps to not only explicitly discuss the benefits of listening patiently but also give students plenty of models for what it looks like. We might, for instance, lead students in a fishbowl activity. This would involve speaking with a colleague or student as the other students observe—and critique— our listening skills. The model conversation could be about anything, but ideally about something our students easily understand, like what happened at recess or a new movie. One speaker might model various patient listening behaviors such as being silent, nodding their head, or making eye contact.

The other speaker would model examples of *impatient* listening, picked from typical student behavior. For instance, kindergartners often learn (if they don't already know it from preschool) that frantically waving their hand gets a reliable response. As they move through elementary school, many students are regularly rewarded in academic spaces for this habit, even though it is antithetical to listening patiently. Raised hands, whether they are still or in constant motion, are a sign that the student's focus is not on the classmate who is speaking. Pointing this out in the modeled conversation will make it clear. (Of course, throughout the year students will still need to be reminded that listening patiently includes putting hands down when someone else is speaking. Matt's high school students need these reminders too!)

The impatient speaker in the fishbowl might model other behaviors, like calling out. Many students, when they agree with or feel a connection to something a classmate says, will be moved to speak without regard to anything else that's going on. Unlike the hand-waving, this habit might never have been encouraged in school, but it may have been encouraged in other conversational spaces. Students may be used to hearing, "Yeah, that's right!" or "I agree!" blurted out, meant to encourage a friend. While well-intentioned, these interjections can also unintentionally *distract* either the speaker or other participants trying to focus on them. This issue, too, becomes clearer when the habit is observed and reflected upon from the outside in—as in a fishbowl.

As conversations continue throughout the school year, it helps to regularly point out how students' behaviors match these early modeling activities. For students who are listening patiently in the moment, this acknowledgment will give them a clear chance to be proud of themselves for mastering a skill (instead of just "being good"). And importantly, students who are not listening patiently in the moment will be reminded of the need to work on it—without the unnecessary disciplinary vibe. They will also be reminded that everyone—teacher included—is spending the year working to get there.

"Okay, let's try it."

Modeling is not enough. As students see what listening patiently both does and doesn't look like, they need low-stakes opportunities to practice the skill. Jen often provides this practice with partner conversations. She knows that talking with only one other classmate means both students get more opportunities to talk than they would in a large group. This lessens kids' urgency to be heard and makes it easier to focus on listening. In order to support students in building their stamina for listening patiently, Jen often starts off these practice conversations with prompts that are both accessible and engaging. She wants students to be all-in on the conversation, both as speakers and as listeners. Allowing students to choose their partners also helps because it means, at least mostly, they will be speaking with someone they like and will thus be more naturally invested in listening to them patiently. The most important part comes after their conversations, in the deliberate reflection, when Jen has students think about what it *felt* like to listen patiently to their partners.

> **Ms. Orr:** *When you were listening to your partner, how did you feel? What did you notice in your body?*

> **Jason:** *I felt like I was looking at Max.*

> **Kennedy:** *I felt kinda fidgety because I wanted to talk.*

Ms. Orr: *Show a thumbs-up if you felt like you were looking at your partner or if you felt fidgety like Kennedy while you waited.*

. . .

Ms. Orr: *I noticed you were nodding at your partner, Heather. Did you feel that?*

Heather: *Yeah, I did!*

Ms. Orr: *Did anyone else notice they were nodding at their partner? . . . Anything else you noticed about how you felt?*

Justin: *I was sitting pretty still. Devon had some really great predictions for the book!*

Ms. Orr: *Thank you, Justin. We can hear some fascinating ideas and questions when we're listening patiently.*

We can also take a moment in these conversations to explore how it felt to be listened to, as that awareness can reinforce for students the power of listening patiently.

Ms. Orr: *Now that you've thought about how you felt while you were waiting to talk, take a moment to think about how you felt when your partner was listening to you.*

Noah: *It felt really good. He was listening, and it felt like what I was saying was good.*

Kylie: *Yeah, it made me feel like what I was saying was really important. Like he was interested in it.*

Fatmata: *It was easier to listen to Heather because she listened to me.*

Ms. Orr: *Wow, when other people listen to us, it is a really powerful feeling. Can you believe you made someone feel that way because you were such a good listener?*

"But how do I hold on to my point?"

Of course, since young children get distracted easily, they may forget what they wanted to say while letting others speak. When that happens, some kids will get upset. They'll feel slighted because they didn't get to share in time and now can't. Hearing a student say, with great frustration, "Great! Now I don't remember what I wanted to say!" can temporarily take the excitement out of an otherwise wonderful classroom conversation. This is when those seconds spent on truthful communication do their heaviest lifting. We can genuinely acknowledge this student's frustration while making it clear that the class has benefitted from hearing classmates who weren't interrupted.

As students begin to recognize the value of listening patiently, and are feeling more comfortable doing so, they'll have more incentive to work on their impulse control and will sincerely try to hold onto their ideas as they listen. But it's still tough. We've all been there. We know that focusing on remembering our points while simultaneously listening to others can be exhausting.

One technique Jen teaches her students is to put one thumb inside their fist when they have an idea they want to share. It's kind of like the old idea of tying a string around a finger to help remember something. The physical act of moving their thumb while thinking about what they want to say helps cement the thought in their mind. If that isn't enough—and a lot of times it isn't—she'll add a bit. She might tell students, "I have an idea that I want to share, but it isn't my turn to talk yet. I'm going to put my thumb inside my fist to help me remember. As I move my thumb [holding up her hand and showing them], I'm going to think, *I want to say . . .* Then, when I kind of wiggle my thumb a bit while I'm waiting, I can remember that while I listen to my friends." The act of holding their fists tight as they hold their ideas tight makes their engagement in the conversation visible. It's not a perfect strategy, but it does help.

Sometimes, throughout this book, we'll pause to explore strategies that might be more appropriate for certain age ranges. Some ideas will be meant for younger elementary students, and some will be more fitting for older elementary students. There are different strategies for helping students hold on to their ideas while they listen, depending on their age and literacy development.

KINDERGARTNERS AND FIRST GRADERS

When Jen needs to remember something, she typically writes herself a short note. In fact, she has nearly a dozen different apps on her phone for exactly this purpose! Kindergartners and first graders don't typically have this luxury, and not just because they're less likely to have phones. Their writing skills are still developing, and the process of figuring out exactly what they want to write, how to spell the words (even if it's spelling by listening to the sounds rather than exact spelling), and then thinking about how the letters are formed is a lot of work. This mental and physical exertion is much more intense for students at this stage than it will be in just a year or two. So they really need other strategies for remembering their points while classmates speak. Young students can draw something, instead of writing it, as a reminder to themselves. (In all honesty, though, even quick drawings or notes don't always help, as sometimes these little ones can't recall what they meant when they put pencil to paper. This will vary greatly by class and by individual student.) One thing that can be quite helpful with our youngest learners is giving them a chance to think and talk through their ideas with one classmate before (or even during a pause in the middle of) a larger group conversation. That can be a great support for remembering their ideas while also helping them organize their thoughts.

SECOND AND THIRD GRADERS

In these middle-elementary grades, students are able to write, but it isn't a quick, easy action yet for many of them. Although they can make a note of their thinking during a conversation in order to remember it, they are unlikely to be able to continue to follow the conversation while they pause to jot down their thought. If it is important to our students to hold on to their ideas while others speak but they struggle to do this independently, we might opt to pause the entire conversation every so often to allow students to write notes to themselves. For example, we might say, "Listening to what Brenda just said reminded me of something that happened to me. I don't want to forget it, so I'm going to make a note to myself. There are a lot of words in my head from what she said. I can't write them all down. I'm going to write just enough to help me remember my thought." Then we can model writing a few words, maybe the name of a person in our memory or the place it happened, whatever might help us remember the bigger idea.

Some students will use this pause to make a note of their own thinking, while others might take that time to process what they've been hearing. For those who need the opportunity to write down their ideas, this strategy can support their independence in a couple of ways. First, the more frequently students stop and jot in this way, the more quickly they'll be able to do it, and they might not always need a pause in the whole-class conversation to make it happen. Of course, it helps if they understand (and truly believe) that these notes don't need correct spelling or punctuation!

Second, stopping to write down their ideas builds students' short-term memory. After some time using this strategy, they may be better able to hold onto their ideas without writing them down, meaning fewer students may need that pause to jot.

FOURTH AND FIFTH GRADERS

By the upper-elementary grades, students are not only able to quickly write down notes to themselves, they are also able to summarize or identify key ideas. As a result, we can teach students in these grades to have a few Post-it notes or a piece of scratch paper with them during conversations and, while the talk continues, to jot down a brief reminder to themselves about what they want to share. We might want to model a think-aloud a few times, pausing during a conversation to say, "I'm thinking that I want to share *this information* [giving them the long idea], but I don't want to interrupt at the moment. So I'll grab my paper and quickly write down these three words to help me remember without missing out on what is still being discussed."

We also have some conversations with these students about the frustration of forgetting an idea. We can affirm students' feelings about it while also reassuring them that they'll have lots of other ideas to share and that they aren't alone in forgetting an idea that was brilliant. It happens to us all.

Practice what we preach!

One quick reminder: we, as the adults, have to listen patiently too. In the busyness and controlled chaos of an elementary classroom, we may find this to be quite a challenge. Our focus is too often on managing the chaos rather than on specific students. Jen knows she tends to jump in rather than wait for students to finish their thought. Young learners may need time to start to share their thinking, pause as they consider what they're saying, rethink a bit, continue, and pause again. It is so easy to step into the silence when they pause and to say, "So you're trying to say . . ." The problem is, whether we're right or wrong, most young kids will agree with whatever we, as the teacher and authority, say.

"UPON FURTHER REFLECTION" on Listening Patiently

In *Not Light*, I wrote declaratively about interrupting: "We don't interrupt for any reason, including affirmations and agreements, both of which still have the unintended effect of drawing focus from the speaker" (Kay 2018, 18). I wanted to make very clear how important it was to train kids to let each other finish their thoughts. I'm a stutterer who, as an elementary-aged kid, was constantly interrupted for seemingly generous reasons (as if to put me out of my stammering Porky Pig misery). So I have a particular passion for this rule. Yet, around midway through 2020, I stumbled onto a few articles about human interruption. A few interesting ideas emerged: The first was that people in different cultures interrupt each other differently. According to research by Han Li, a professor of psychology at the University of Northern British Columbia in Canada, "Chinese speakers tend to interrupt each other more often with 'cooperative interruptions' such as agreeing with what was said or providing assistance with a word or idea, than with 'intrusive interruptions', such as attempts to steal the floor or change the subject" (Burrell 2018). Canadian speakers, on the other hand were found to use slightly more intrusive interruptions. The second interesting idea was the possible influence of gender on interrupting.

Georgetown professor of linguistics Deborah Tannen found that while women interrupt each other more than men do, they do so "cooperatively," whereas men do it "intrusively." These findings, and more, have added some color to *Not Light*'s absolutist take on interrupting—to a point. I am still certain that, in most cases, students shouldn't interrupt each other. However, Jen and I also encourage you to engage interrupting with both a respect for cultural competency and an understanding of how complex the habit might be. We should understand that, for some students, the expectation that they let their classmates finish might seem like an overcorrection. (For example, a student might interrupt a classmate who was grasping for a word, get critiqued by a teacher for it, then think, "Where I'm from, we interrupt to help each other out, and it brings us closer together. You're only making me stop because it bothers some of *you*.") We must explain *why* we are coaching them to be patient—not because the habit is automatically rude, not because one culture's values on interrupting are inherently better than another's, but because in a collaborative setting—sometimes with many cultures participating—*not* interrupting establishes an important baseline: *all* focus goes to the speaker. When kids speak, it's safe for them to count on being the main attraction.

LISTEN ACTIVELY

When students are *listening actively*, they are not just showing the speaker that they are paying close attention (listening patiently); they are also *thoughtfully engaging* with the ideas being shared. Students demonstrate active listening in a number of ways, such as by citing each other's contributions to the class discussion and by asking each other thoughtful questions that seek understanding.

Once young children recognize the power of listening to others and are practicing it regularly, it's much easier for them to authentically engage the ideas they're hearing from classmates. In many elementary classrooms, we have already developed ways to quickly identify students who are listening actively. Jen, for instance, teaches kids to make the "connection sign," sticking out both thumb and pinky and moving their hand between themself and the person speaking. This signals to the speaker that the listener "connects" with what is being said.

Another habit that inspires active listening requires only a slight change in a teacher's prompting. Early in the school year (and ongoing throughout the year as necessary), Jen has students share out after partner conversations—but not their own ideas. She'll ask, "Did anyone hear something really interesting *from their partner*?" or "What did *your partner* share that you think the whole class should hear?" It takes only a few instances of sharing out this way before students are as focused on retaining their partner's ideas as they are on retaining their own. Eventually, when Jen simply asks, "Does anyone want to share out from their partner [or small group] conversation?" students more naturally share their own ideas *and* the ideas they have heard.

Modeling is just as important for teaching active listening as it is for teaching patient listening. It can be simpler, though. To show students how it might look to listen actively, we just label certain ideas (that is, we say which student said them) and remember to use this citation whenever we refer back to these (or similar) ideas.

> **Hannah:** *I was thinking that Maya [in Jacqueline Woodson's* Each Kindness*] was feeling hurt because the other girls wouldn't play with her.*

> **Ms. Orr:** *So you were thinking about a character's emotions in this book.*

> **Logan:** *I think Chloe was mean. She didn't treat Maya like she would want to be treated.*

> **Ms. Orr:** *You're thinking about a character trait, Logan.*

> **Valentina:** *Maya was mean, but I think she felt bad at the end of the book.*

Ms. Orr: *You were noticing a character's emotions, Valentina.*
Just like Hannah was.

Something as simple as noting how one student's thinking is related to another student's thinking helps our young learners do the same. It shows them that we are actively listening to the *content* of speakers' contributions and that we value them. If we, as adults, value students' specific ideas, students will often believe these same ideas have value.

It is also helpful to teach students some language to use when they engage each others' ideas. In conversations early in the school year, we can remind our youngest children (kindergarten through second grade) to say "I agree" or "I disagree" in response to an idea they have heard.

> If we, as adults, value students' specific ideas, students will often believe these same ideas have value.

Agreeing and disagreeing with their classmates' ideas shows that, at the simplest level, they are listening to the speaker—not just being quiet. From here, we grow to adding "because" to the end of the "I agree/disagree" statement and including more of the students' own reasoning. With older students we can offer more complex sentence starters. We might suggest that these students say something like "Hearing Ashley's thinking makes me think . . ." or maybe "Now that Ashley said that, I'm thinking . . ." In this way, they may be agreeing and disagreeing, but they are also building upon their classmate's idea, adding to our conversation.

As with listening patiently, it matters that we teachers listen actively too. Jen is confident that all her active listening over the years has helped her teach her students more effectively. Students' questions often illustrate confusion that is an unintended result of instruction, such as when Jen's students once asked her whether George Washington and Abraham Lincoln had been friends. This taught her that teaching history from one big event to another might not give young children an understanding of how time moves. At other times, students will remark on things about a lesson that they enjoyed—or that surprised them—providing useful insight into their experiences. When we listen actively to our students, we gain a deeper understanding of their thinking, and we are better prepared to help them continue growing. Our students often value whatever they see us valuing, and when we show that we are not just being patient but are actually collecting and engaging their ideas, they experience first-hand what it truly means to be present in a scholarly community. And they learn that it is important.

"UPON FURTHER REFLECTION" on Listening Actively

In *Not Light*, I focused on encouraging our students to build upon each other's comments. I described a few ways that I've done this, like tracking *who says an idea and what additional ideas that first idea inspires* on the board for all to see. In professional development sessions, I tend to describe first encouraging, then requiring students to cite each other's contributions to class discussions in analytical essays. However, conversations with teachers have driven me to deeper reflection about *why* it can be so difficult for students to authentically engage each other's ideas. While hurdles include the many digital distractions students must navigate, there are deeper challenges. Most prominent among them is the "cognitive load" that such intensive listening puts on our students. According to cognitive load research, humans' "working memory" (our personal RAM) is limited: adult thinkers can retain seven items (or fewer) in our working memory for anywhere from fifteen seconds to a minute (Birnbaum 2018), while young children can retain less, and for a shorter amount of time (Dewar 2019). This has real implications for young students' active listening, especially in whole-class conversations, when the focus and topic might switch unexpectedly. By tracking a conversation's thread of relevant responses for the class, the teacher can release a portion of students' cognitive load, as students no longer need to retain a comment that is now available on the board, or in the chat box, or wherever the teacher has captured it. This strategy also eases the transition from working memory to long-term memory by helping our students organize the relevant information in their classmates' comments into schemas (Stern

2019). Making students' thinking visible in some way increases the likelihood that they will apply what they have learned from each other in the conversation to new contexts.

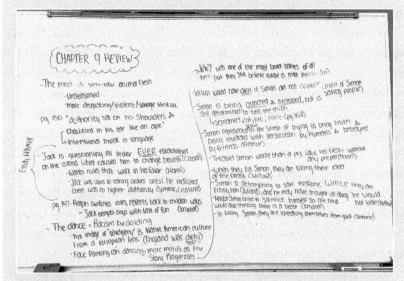

FIGURE 1.1
Matt's notes jotted down during a conversation to help students track ideas. This same strategy is useful in elementary school as well.

CONTROL YOUR VOICE

When students are *controlling their voices*, they are noticing the space they are taking up in the class conversation and then making sure that they are leaving space for others to share. This work involves students developing their mental clocks and sharpening their awareness of social cues.

It can feel overwhelming to think about helping six- or nine- or eleven-year-olds learn to control their voices. On the positive side, elementary students frequently feel strongly about things being fair and will get on board with this goal, once they understand it! It is also important to recognize that, like some adults, some children are going to have a lot to say and will want to share again and again, while others are going to be more hesitant and more likely to listen. Speaking and listening are both valuable in our classroom conversations. The goal is to ensure that *all* students have the space and opportunity to share and be heard.

As elementary school teachers, we can all name that student, the one we never call on when there's only a minute or two left before heading to lunch because we know we *won't* make it on time if we do. It can seem as if those students just like the sound of their own voices, but there's often much more to it. They might be using their talk-time to figure out exactly what they think, something we (Jen and Matt) are frequently guilty of doing ourselves. It's hard for these students to be succinct in those moments because they honestly don't know what they're trying to say. They are figuring it out *as* they talk. It helps to suggest that these students consciously pause for a few seconds after being called on to get their thoughts organized. In some conversations, we might have them do some writing or drawing before the talk begins.

Other students ramble because, after they would naturally be finished speaking, they start reading our facial expressions and body language to see if they're "right" (whatever "right" might look like in that moment). These students now keep talking, hoping to see us give the visual cue that says they've "got it." Elementary teachers often work for years to develop a poker face that, while broadly encouraging students, works to decrease their reliance on visual feedback from us to know when they are "right." This requires self-awareness on our part, as we all have different quirks in body language and speech habits when leading conversations. If, for instance, we tend to nod at the "end" of student comments, students might habitually speak until they get that nod. The same is true if we tend to say "Okay!" or "Nice!" or other subtle affirmations. The lack of affirmation any one time might cause some kids to keep speaking until they get it.

There are many more reasons why students might overtalk. But helping them learn to do it less almost always begins with the same approach—reflection.

Early on in our conversations, it's important that we talk with the class about making sure everyone has an opportunity to be an active participant.

We should remind students that we can only listen actively when we are not talking. For that reason, we should try to limit the length of our comments so that we can get back to listening to our classmates. After conversations we might ask, "How do you feel about how much you got to talk today? Hold up your hand. A one means you are not happy at all with how much you got to talk, a three means you're fine with it, and a five means you feel great about it." We might then say, "Look around. Notice how many people feel great or fine about how much they talked. For those of you who don't feel so good, what could we do in future conversations to make it better for you?" Young students may not have an answer for that, and we may need to offer them some suggestions. Older elementary students frequently do have ideas, though. They'll often say that they need others to talk less frequently or for shorter amounts of time. Hearing from their classmates what they can do is often more meaningful for students than hearing it from an adult.

For some students, however, simply providing peer feedback and directing their attention to it won't completely resolve the challenges. In a typical elementary classroom, it will be pretty obvious just a few weeks into the year which students want to share all the time. If one or two of those students don't respond to reminders about controlling their voices and giving other students the chance to participate, they might need a private conversation, followed up with some coaching. While others are reading or writing independently, Jen might sit down with a student and talk about the challenges of controlling their voice.

Ms. Orr: *Hey, Katherine, you have lots of great ideas and questions to share in our conversations. I've noticed you have your hand raised a lot. Your thinking can help us see something in a new way. I have also noticed that sometimes it's hard for you to control your voice and to give others a chance to speak.*

Katherine: *I know! I try but I have so many thoughts in my head!*

Ms. Orr: *I can tell! Do you have ideas for strategies that might help you control your voice? Or would you like me to suggest some possibilities?*

Katherine: *I don't know. I feel like I'm really doing my best.*

29

Ms. Orr: *You know it's something you have to work on, and that's great. One thing you might try is deciding how many times you're going to talk in a conversation. Let's say you pick three times. Put out three fingers when the conversation starts and each time you talk, put one finger down. If you still have things you really want to say after you run out of fingers, you can write them down to remember them for another time.*

Strategies for students who are finding it hard to control their voices can look very different. While not all students will need or respond well to the suggestion above, it is one Jen frequently offers kids who speak often. Other students may not speak again and again, but when they do speak, they can be long-winded. Coaching these students might look different.

Ms. Orr: *Max, during our conversations you often have a really interesting idea to share, and your classmates benefit from hearing your thinking. Sometimes, it seems that when you share, you talk for a while, making it more challenging for your friends to have a chance to talk too. Do you have any thoughts about why that is happening?*

Max: *Not really. It just takes a bit for me to say what I'm thinking.*

Ms. Orr: *That happens to me sometimes too. I have a thought and I start to talk about it. Then, while I'm talking, I kind of change my thinking or add on and so I keep talking. Does it feel that way?*

Max: *I guess so, yeah.*

Ms. Orr: *Maybe you could try this: How about if you start to talk, then pause to take a deep breath and think about the one big thing you want to share. After you share that one big thing, you might have other ideas, of course! You can give others a chance to share and then come back into the conversation to share your next thought. What do you think?*

In Jen's experience, the majority of elementary students can control their voices with a few gentle reminders. If necessary, we can always return to the concept of fairness. We can remind students that by keeping their own talk reasonably short and giving others a turn, they are truly sharing the space and being fair to their classmates.

"UPON FURTHER REFLECTION" on Controlling Your Voice

This rule was called "Police Your Voice" in *Not Light*, which came out in 2018. The brutal 2020 murder of George Floyd under the knee of Minneapolis police officer Derek Chauvin prompted a few nervous emails from colleagues around the country, asking if it would be best for them to find a substitute for the word "police," given the negative connotations saturating the media at the time (in addition to the very real association between police and state-sanctioned racialized violence that is so raw in many communities). My answer remains "Maybe." If you've read *Not Light* and feel that the word "police" will be a distraction to your students, or even a trigger that causes them pain, then yes. Absolutely. This is why we've changed the term here, just to make this flexibility clear. It's our job to take care of our students, and that includes being sensitive to the loaded nature of certain words and phrases. However, while it's far from the hill I'm dying on, I do stand by *Not Light*'s original wording, if teachers, knowing their kids, choose to use it. We *do* want students to learn to "control, regulate, and keep the order of" their own voice in our scholarly discussions—a common definition of the transitive verb "to police." A few teachers have suggested substitutes like "monitor your voice" and "manage your airtime," which come close but, in my opinion, don't quite capture the varied and complex skills we want young people to be developing.

In addition to simply "monitoring" whether or not they are overtalking—certainly an important step in its own right—students getting ready for meaningful race conversations should also gradually become more aware of intersections between their identities, their lived experience, and their relative expertise on the topics being discussed. And we want them to *use* this awareness to determine which of their classmates' voices should be centered, when to talk, and when to *stop* talking. Let's say the class is discussing an immigration issue. Students who don't have an immigrant experience should not drown out the voices of those who do. If they notice that a classmate with relevant life experience is trying to speak—and there is limited time—they should make sure that they step aside to make room. If they find that their voice really doesn't want to stop speeding, students need to do more than just "monitor" it; they need to hit the metaphorical sirens and *make* it pull over. Be in (self) control. (Self) regulate. A student who fully "gets it" might even preface opinions about topics they aren't intimately familiar with by owning that they might not be an expert. You might hear a student say, "I *think* the other kids didn't like Maya and bullied her [in *Each Kindness*] because she seemed poor. Her clothes weren't nice, and she seemed kind of dirty. But I don't know for sure, because I haven't seen kids like that." How many adults do we wish had started on the pathway toward both developing and acting upon this self-awareness as young students?

SPEAK TO EACH OTHER AS "FAMILY" (OR AT LEAST AS "FAMILY ADJACENT")

Establishing a classroom culture that teaches and practices authentic listening might lead to seismic change. But listening patiently, listening actively, and controlling our voices alone won't make any classroom fully ready for meaningful race conversations. In addition to authentic listening, these conversations also require vulnerability, bravery, and humility—attributes rarely expected of students during class discussions. This big ask (and in some conversations, it can be massive) is often easier to carry out among people who share certain lived experiences or cultural understandings. For instance, it would be hubristic of Matt to assume that girls should be automatically eager to share stories about street harassment with him. They *might* prefer sharing with Jen, for whom some things common to a woman's experience might not need to be explained. (She is also clearly less likely to bring an irritating #NotAllMen self-congratulatory tone to the exchange.) Similarly, it would be hubristic of Jen to assume that students of color would be automatically eager to share how it feels when their families lose homes as their neighborhoods gentrify. They *might* prefer sharing with Matt, for whom some things common to certain Black experiences need not be explained. In both cases, we might even erroneously think that because a kid eats lunch in our room, laughs at our corny jokes, or has a special handshake with us, they are eager to engage with us in the exclusive, intimate, honest discourse that Matt's family cheekily calls "house talk." But, as Matt wrote in *Not Light,*

> there has always been a difference between collegial banter and *house talk*, between the water cooler and the dining room table. It is dangerous to invite ourselves to the latter because we are tolerated at the former. We must, if we value our students' right to determine healthy relationships, never accept invitations unless they have been proffered. We must, through earnest humility, earn our seats.
>
> *(Kay 2018, 29)*

And perhaps even more importantly, we must set up situations where our students can do the same with each other.

Not Light described three activities that Matt has used to build and maintain house talk relationships among his secondary students over the years. Here, Jen will share two that have worked well for her elementary students. Before reading further, though, it's important that you understand that these activities are merely suggestions. You know your kids. Feel free to both find and create house talk activities that work best with them. The crucial thing is that these activities are routinized, given their own special place in our pedagogy, and are *never* an afterthought or something exclusive to "extra" time.

Morning Meeting

For nearly two decades now, Jen's students have started every day with a Morning Meeting. The most common structure for Morning Meeting comes from Responsive Classroom (Responsive Classroom 2016). It begins with a greeting, continues with some kind of share time followed by a group activity, and ends with a message the teacher has written for the class. This is a daily routine that is focused on Jen's class being a community together. It is a positive, fun, thoughtful shared experience every single day. Not only is it daily, but it is the first thing the class does together. Its importance in the day is clear, and it results in stronger conversations throughout the year (Banse, Curby, Palacios, and Rimm-Kaufman 2018).

The structure and details of Jen's Morning Meetings have varied based on the age of her students and new things she's learned, but it has always been a crucial part of every day. The students gather on the carpet together, in a circle (or some proximity of one), and start off with a greeting, a chance to say hello to one another and start their day as a community. That's followed by time for sharing, a group activity, and a message (a short note from Jen that may give information about the day or week and offers students opportunities to practice reading and word study skills). The share time is something Jen purposely keeps very open and broad, except for very specific times of the year (the day after a break or Halloween, for example, they'll do a lightning share, giving every student a quick chance, because young children often *all* want to share in those moments). Every student can share at least once a week, and they can share about anything they want.

They often share about the sports they are playing, a birthday of a family member or friend, their pet, or what they're going to do after school. They share whatever is at the top of their mind. That does mean that they sometimes share hard or sad parts of their lives. This kind of sharing is a sign of their trust in the community, and their classmates are likely to respond with empathy and support. In these moments, our first instinct may be to jump in and address whatever has been shared. Jen's experience, however, has taught her the value of pausing. Some students just need to share and say the difficult thing out loud. Others will get all they need from their classmates' responses. One student shared that a baby who lived nearby, in a family that was close to hers, had died. She was clearly upset. Her classmates immediately told her how sad that was and asked her how she was feeling. That connection with her friends seemed to do a lot to support her and help her get through the morning. (Jen did follow up with her after Morning Meeting and also reached out to the school counselor so they'd be ready if the student needed them.) In these moments, whether what is shared is big and heavy or light and fun, it's almost possible to see the sparks of meaningful connections shooting around our room.

This share time during Morning Meeting doesn't just connect Jen's students to one another, although it does that very well. It also allows Jen to get to know her students in ways that she otherwise might not in the course of the school day. Hearing about their families, their lives outside of school, and the challenges or hardships they are facing helps Jen better understand her students and be better prepared to support them. Jen herself doesn't usually share (although she'll participate when they do lightning shares), but she does sometimes ask questions. If there are lots of classmates with questions, she stays back and gives them the floor. If, however, there aren't a lot of questions, Jen might raise her hand and ask something about what was shared. At other times, Jen might ask students about their share at different points in the day, maybe at recess or during a reading or writing conference. Showing that she's listening and interested in what they share makes her care for her students visible.

FIGURE 1.2
A chart from Jen's classroom showing the components of the Morning Meeting

While sharing is the most obvious aspect of Morning Meeting when it comes to house talk, the three other components (greeting, activity, and message) are all helpful too. Jen reflects frequently on the greetings, activities, and messages used in her Morning Meetings. She wants to be sure the options she is choosing from are as focused on strengthening our relationships as they are on academic content. She also wants to be sure the choices are resonating with her students. She avoids activities that are competitive and identify winners and losers, instead opting for ones that require the group to work together or are just plain fun. For her messages, she writes about events in the classroom, the school, or the community—or she connects to historical events. She wants the message to highlight shared experiences or help students gain shared knowledge, without adding extra anxiety by making it about academics.

Jen's students also run the Morning Meeting, which helps the community come together. For the first month or so of the school year, Jen is the Meeting Manager. In that time, students learn the four components (greeting, activity, share, and message), practice different greetings and activities, and basically get the routine down. Then, Meeting Manager becomes a daily job. It rotates every day, and every student gets that job every month or so. That means a student picks and leads the greeting, calls on classmates for share time, picks and leads the activity, and reads the morning message. Elementary students thrive on having such responsibility. Being Meeting Managers also shows students that they have ownership in the classroom. That is something elementary students don't always feel. Owning a piece of the day, a time when the teacher participates just like a student and a student takes the traditional role of the teacher, is powerful in the eyes of a six- or nine-year-old. It changes how they see themselves as a part of the classroom community.

Interactive read-alouds

Another house talk activity that Jen uses regularly is an interactive read-aloud. At least three times a week she reads a picture book to her students, stopping deliberately at planned points to allow for discussion. Early in the year she chooses books that she expects her elementary students to have lots of ideas about. That might mean books with characters they can easily relate to or characters who will make them laugh or get angry. It might mean books with lots of cliffhanger points at which to deliberately stop and discuss. She also reads longer books on a daily basis, a chapter or two per day. As the year goes on, these interactive read-alouds are linked more directly to the language arts curriculum, but the primary purpose remains to build relationships.

Think about attending a movie, concert, or play. Even if you don't know anyone else there, you feel a sense of connection through that shared experience. Read-alouds are another shared experience. Students bond as a class as they live vicariously through the characters in their books. As Pam Allyn writes in "Creating Community by Reading Aloud":

> the experience of reading aloud is a profound exchange—the company of one another in the experience, to talk about the text, to marvel over a riveting excerpt, to laugh together over a funny part, or to cry over something sad. These are all emotions that, when shared with someone else, create a bond wrapped in empathy and a love for reading. It is part of a lifelong journey of reading and sharing experiences to learn about the world.
>
> *(Allyn 2021)*

During these interactive read-alouds, students share their thinking and frequently make connections between their lives and the book. The vulnerability that students exhibit during these discussions shows a teacher how well they are developing trust in one another. Students give their classmates a new window into who they are, which gives everyone new ways to connect. These connections often bloom into friendships.

Many of Jen's favorite read-alouds are books that involve sibling or family issues. Every year she reads Rukhsana Khan's *Big Red Lollipop*, about a Pakistani-American family. The oldest sister gets invited to a birthday party, and the mother insists that she take her younger sister with her. Doing so, not surprisingly, goes very badly. After the party, the younger sister eats or breaks everything in her goodie bag while the older sister saves her big red lollipop. In the morning, she finds that her younger sister has eaten her lollipop, and she is very angry. Eventually, the younger sister gets invited to her first birthday party, and the mother insists she take both of her sisters with her. The oldest convinces her mother not to do that. After her younger sister goes to the party alone, she brings a big lollipop home to her big sister. This book always gets students sharing thoughts and experiences:

- "My mom always makes me take my little brother with me! Everywhere I go!"

- "I totally take things from my big sister. Mostly she doesn't notice!" Followed by a sly smile and giggle.

- "We played musical chairs at my friend's birthday party, just like in the book!"

- "My big sister is totally mean to me. Rubina was really nice to her little sister."

These shared experiences around books come back again and again throughout the year. As we talk about new books or as we work to problem-solve as a class, students will use previous reads as sources of examples and ideas. Jen might hear, "Remember CJ's nana in *Last Stop on Market Street*? Remember how she could always find the positive. I bet we can find the positive in not getting to have specials this week because of testing." Jen's young students have these books as touchpoints they return to as needed. The books link the students and give all parties a common language and a common understanding of their community.

> These shared experiences around books come back again and again throughout the year.

SHIFTING OUR THINKING AROUND MISTAKES

There are a few concrete reasons that some subjects are theoretically easier to discuss within our families (or shared cultural communities) than outside of them. One is that fewer "basic" cultural elements might need to be explained before getting to the meat of the conversation. Another is that, as we just mentioned, we have already made strong connections with these people in our own circles, we know what experiences we share, and we are therefore more likely to trust each other moment to moment. A third reason flows naturally from this: with family, it's (again, theoretically) a little easier to make "mistakes." We've all heard some version of "Well, even after all that, she's still my sister." While our students may never get *that* close with each other, we've got to get them close *enough*. If students are going to take risks—which conversations about potentially heavy topics like race often require—we've got to fundamentally change the way our students handle each other's "mistakes" (and the way we, their teachers, handle both theirs and our own).

Jen has clear memories of her first few years of teaching, when making a mistake felt like such a shameful thing. She can recall how, when she misspelled something on the whiteboard or called a student by the wrong name or gave the wrong answer to a math problem, her face would flush, she would stumble, and she'd do all she could to cover up the error. The sense that she couldn't make mistakes in front of her students was very strong.

Fortunately, Jen eventually realized that not allowing her students to see her mistakes inadvertently sent them a message that they too should hide their mistakes. Her first step forward was publicly accepting her mistakes, saying to her students, "Oops, I misspelled that. Let me fix it," or "Oh my goodness, you're totally right. That wasn't the correct answer. Thank you for pointing that out to me." When we let our students see us make mistakes, recognize our mistakes, and keep moving forward, we give them a model for doing the same. They can, hopefully, begin to build a mindset of seeing mistakes as everyday occurrences, not something to get upset about.

Then we can go one step further. We can *celebrate* mistakes. Research has shown that our brains are growing when we make mistakes. "Mistakes are not only opportunities for learning, as students consider the mistakes, but also times when our brains grow, even if we don't know we have made a mistake" (Boaler 2022, 12). What a powerful idea for our students to understand! A classroom in which students see mistakes as opportunities to learn is a classroom in which students will take more risks. And taking risks is critical to engaging in meaningful conversations.

We can teach our students, even our youngest elementary learners, about how mistakes help their brains grow. Then we can identify mistakes and celebrate brain growth. When a student makes a mistake in our classrooms, we can respond with "Can you feel your brain growing? You're getting new synapses right now!" In our experience, it doesn't take long before students begin telling each other and themselves about their brain growth when they notice a mistake.

Creating a classroom full of people—adults and students—who are willing to engage in difficult conversations is no small feat. Changing our view of mistakes and then helping our students do the same is one way to support such an environment.

INVITE FAMILIES INTO HOUSE TALK

One clear difference between teaching at the secondary and elementary levels is the degree to which parents pay attention to the curriculum and the teacher's pedagogical practices (that is, at least, until our country's recent surge of book banning and anti-CRT hysteria). By the time their children reach high school, many parents have started to trust them to tackle school mostly on their own. Parents of younger children, however, rightfully pay close attention to their students' day-to-day school life, concerned about their early development as learners. This means that there are

> Parents' home values must be humbly acknowledged. Their concerns must not be casually dismissed.

more parent eyes on the schoolwork and documents that come home during the elementary school years than what Matt generally sees with his ninth and tenth graders. This level of parental involvement is necessary and good, as young children lean on these supports as they learn how to "do school."

However, this reality complicates our mission to lead meaningful classroom conversations about race, mostly because nearly all elementary curriculum is sure to have most parents' eyes on it. While Matt can send a reading home and feel fairly certain that his students' parents will not casually read it, Jen can *never* make that assumption. While Matt can assume that his students' parents are not likely to grill them about what was learned in one of five or six classes on any given day, Jen must recognize the reality that many parents are certain to ask their second or third graders, "So what did you learn in school today?" This increased attention means that elementary school teachers must do everything they can to keep parents on board. Therefore, they must make sure that the house talk umbrella has ample space for their partners at home. Parents' home values must be humbly acknowledged. Their concerns must not be casually dismissed. Every effort must be made to invite them into important conversations, to encourage them to contribute their talents and energies to supplement their kids' dialogic learning.

THERE ARE MANY WAYS TO INVITE THEM IN

Listening Conferences: In Jen's school, they do listening conferences before the school year begins. They meet one-on-one with each family so caregivers can teach about their child. Classroom teachers ask about the child's strengths and interests, important people in their life, how they cope with frustration, and what the family sees as their hopes and goals for the year. It starts the year off establishing that teachers and families are partners.

Positive Notes Home: Jen sends positive and encouraging emails and makes positive phone calls throughout the year.

Invitations to the Classroom: Jen invites families into the classroom during the second week of school to participate in a Morning Meeting with the class. Then she invites them in once a month all year, at different times of the day, to read with the class, play math games with them, or do a science experiment with them, or for students to share their recent writing.

Private Social Media Groups: By creating a private online group that families can access, Jen shares a window into her classrooms. Being welcoming and open with families sets up a culture of trust.

Regular Class Blogs or Newsletters: After 2020 and 2021, welcoming families into our classrooms has become even more critical than it was before. Because teaching in many school districts was virtual during that time, families, especially those with younger students, were literally a part of our classrooms. Many families will now expect more communication, more information, and more access to their children's daily lives at school. While we can't possibly offer the kind of access they had in virtual schooling, some connection will go a long way toward creating a community that will work together when things get challenging.

In Jen's newsletter, she might share a few highlights of a recent class conversation. At first, those highlights might be focused on how students are making connections with each other, the ways they are supporting and developing their social and emotional skills and adjusting to a new school year. Then it might become more about the conversations around the learning and the content, helping families see how talk is an important part of the learning process. *In this way, families see the importance of talk in our classrooms and the positive impact it has on their students' academic and social skills.*

Emails Explaining How They Can Help: Often, families can continue important conversations at home, especially when the topic is the students' own culture. Emails home can let parents know that their children might be coming home with research to gather or rich questions to explore over the dinner table. They can even be encouraged to bring a conversation up,

I've also attached the last two weeks of our morning messages and activities. You'll see we've been exploring contractions and practicing a variety of math and language skills. We also had really thoughtful conversations about Constitution Day and the  Emancipation Proclamation. Students had a lot of questions about who did and did not have the right to participate in our government at different points in our history. They also shared a lot of thoughts based on things they've learned in second grade, connecting Rosa Parks and Martin Luther King, Jr. to our conversation, as well as family visits to memorials and monuments in Washington, D.C. By chance, we're also reading Joseph Bruchac's Rez Dogs together (it's a novel written in poetry form so it's perfect for our current poetry unit) and students are making connections to the history of native peoples in the United States as well. I am so impressed by their thoughtfulness. They are listening carefully and respectfully to one another and they are adding to and revising their understanding as they do so.

FIGURE 1.3
Example of a family newsletter

in case their children forget to do so. (Chapter 4's class conversation about the cultural significance of names will illustrate this point.)

Communication with the Wider School Community: It's easy to focus on your students and their families as you do the work of inviting them in. It's important to invite in your school administration as well. Purposefully including them in your thinking about your community will be helpful if (when) you face any pushback from families. If you are concerned about that possibility, you definitely want to have some conversations with your administration proactively.

Conversations About Your District's Policies Around Diversity and Equity: Engaging in a conversation with your administration about district policies will help you uncover any misconceptions, on your part or theirs, about doing this work.

If your district has publicly stated support for diversity and equity efforts, know the language used and how it supports specific instructional decisions you are making.

Knowing the Standards That Support Your Instruction: It is critical that you know which grade-level standards align and intersect with the conversations that are a part of your instruction, and you can talk with your administration to determine how they will (or will not) support you if families get upset. This will help your administration support you. If the work you are doing in your classroom is clearly linked to your district's objectives and the standards you teach, it will be harder for anyone to argue against your decisions. Not impossible, just harder.

KEEP YOUR RESUME UPDATED

Sometimes it all just won't work. You might teach in communities that do not believe that certain narratives deserve to be *listened patiently* to. You will try to get students to *control their voices* but find out that their parents shouted down the principal at a board meeting. You'll throw open the doors in an attempt to bring people into your house talk, but nobody will come in. You might even see picketers outside, with your name roughly scrawled on placards and raised above an angry crowd. It's a hard truth that some communities are not ready. It doesn't make any teacher feel good to admit it, especially if you teach where you grew up, where you are raising your children, where you have built your life. We want to acknowledge the very real pain that accompanies this realization. And we need you to know that we are *not* asking you to leap into no-man's-land again and again. Sometimes you will need to retreat. Matt is often asked by colleagues around the country, "But what should a teacher do when people just don't *want* to learn?" We're not being flippant when we answer, "Keep your resume updated."

If we want to teach truth, we sometimes have to leave. We might need to leave a school, or a district, or even a city. It's not a popular sentiment in this culture that celebrates teachers' martyrdom, but it *is* a kind and honest one. Some learning spaces will force us to make compromises that we just aren't willing to make. Members of some communities will dig in and say, "This is who we are, and we are proud of it. If you don't like it, you can go." And you know what? You can. As Matt often tells student teachers, there are kids everywhere. And they *all* deserve the best of you. If your current teaching environment throws up too many roadblocks, don't break your spirit against them. It's not "quitting" to go and be a blessing elsewhere.

CHAPTER 2

DEVELOPING OUR "TALKING GAME"

It's ridiculously easy for good teachers to ruin classroom race conversations. We can have the best relationships with our students, built and fortified by disciplined listening norms and lively house talk activities, and still hurt our students. We can select powerful texts by diverse authors that tackle the thorniest race issues in developmentally appropriate ways, and then proceed to lead a conversation about them that sends students to recess feeling alienated. Our worst lessons—the ones that keep us up at night—might have started the day as sound lesson *plans*, infused with the most powerful dialogical techniques. But *something* happened to make it all go wrong.

That often unexamined *something*, Matt discovered while writing *Not Light*, is an educator's underdeveloped communication skills. Making sure that students are hearing what we intend for them to hear, that they are understanding what we intend for them to understand and are actually feeling the way we *think* they are feeling, this is the skill—or, more precisely, *set* of skills—that can either do our thoughtful plans justice or sink them entirely. We must both reflect upon and work on these subtle—and personal—communication skills with the same energy that we bring to the other, more attention-grabbing elements of our craft.

Before moving on in this chapter, we want to acknowledge the many folks who have cautioned teachers to be aware of the difference between *intent* and *impact* (White 2021). Knowing that "I didn't *mean* to cause any harm" is never an excuse for causing harm is a necessary starting place. However, "intent versus impact" can also be an unfortunately common, oversimplified cudgel used to batter teachers who make mistakes. In this chapter, we don't want to join those who weaponize this phrase. We want to wedge into that vague space between the two terms, and show how to make sure that the latter reliably matches the former in our classroom race conversations.

IDENTITY WORK

As we set students up for a race conversation, it is important to pause and reflect on our own knowledge, journey, and identity in relation to the work we plan to do with students. In *Start Here, Start Now: A Guide to Antibias and Antiracist Work in Your School Community*, Liz Kleinrock recommends that teachers themselves create identity maps before asking their students to engage in identity work (2021). These maps are one way to begin considering how we (our knowledge, our experiences) will impact the race conversation. It is critical to do this work—to consider who we are and how that impacts how we approach others and the world—*before* we engage students in conversations about their own identities.

Identity maps have been and are being used in many fields. Two Canadian researchers, Danielle Jacobson and Nida Mustafa, explored how these maps have become crucial for researchers. They wrote, "These factors—whether one is young, old, a woman, a man, nonbinary, cisgender, trans, a Canadian, an Emirati, White, Black, lower middle class, wealthy, able, with a disability, heterosexual, homosexual, pansexual, and so on—affect the way that we see and interpret the world around us, and how the world sees and interprets us" (2019, 2). In their work, they created identity maps with three tiers. The first tier mirrors what Kleinrock uses with her students. It involves choosing labels for your identity: gender, race, religion, and such. Tier 2 requires you to identify how those aspects of your identity impact your life. Finally, Tier 3 explores the emotions linked to each aspect of identity and its impact. Creating an identity map for ourselves, possibly even as part of a team of like-minded colleagues, is likely to impact our interactions with students and their families. At the very least, we are more likely to approach the writing of our discussion prompts with the requisite humility.

PROMPTS, A QUICK INTRODUCTION

Prompts—short statements that encourage conversation and thought—are the building blocks of dialogic pedagogy. Each prompt serves a different purpose: some kick the conversation off, some push our students' thinking, some gently redirect a conversation that has gone off course, some encourage students to connect their lived experience to a text, some send them home with something to think about. In this chapter, we're going to focus on the two types of prompts most connected to a teacher's communication skills in race conversations. The others we'll address in Chapter 3.

Prompts that get us into race conversations

It matters which prompts we use to enter race conversations. Many classroom communication failures come either from not adequately preparing students for a discussion or from overpreparing them. Discerning the appropriate form of orientation is a skill we'll be working on for the rest of our careers. It goes beyond the need to pique our students' interest. If there is a heavy lift ahead, we want to gird them. If prior knowledge or relevant skills need to be activated, we need to activate them—and do so without *overemphasizing* this prior knowledge and alienating students who haven't yet heard of what we'll be discussing.

There are a couple of things to keep in mind when prompting elementary students at the beginning of a conversation. One, to quote Aaron Burr in *Hamilton*, is to "talk less, smile more." It is very easy, as a teacher of young children, to find ourselves talking *at* them a lot. To give a lot of directions and repeat them much too often. To frontload a lot of background knowledge. Pretty quickly, to them, we sound like the adults in the old Charlie Brown videos: "Wah wah, wah wah wah wah."

Avoiding this pattern requires that we:

1. Trust young students to engage in a race conversation even if they have a limited range of background knowledge.

47

2. Trust in the process of our conversation itself to support their learning.

3. Trust ourselves to jump in when necessary to support students.

From this confident starting place, we can begin to craft thoughtful "warm-up" prompts, questions that give students the chance to be thoughtful, think critically, ask questions, and construct their understanding together. There are a number of things to keep in mind when writing them.

WARM-UP PROMPTS MAY VARY SIGNIFICANTLY DEPENDING ON STUDENTS' AGE AND THE RACIAL AND ETHNIC MAKEUP OF OUR STUDENT POPULATION.

Some of our kindergartners and first graders may not have a lot of experience or background knowledge when it comes to issues of race. As students get a little older and have more personal experience and more opportunities to gather background knowledge, the orientation for a race conversation may look less like providing the foundation for the discussion and more like preparing students for a challenge.

WARM-UP PROMPTS SHOULD ENCOURAGE STUDENTS TO QUESTION AND CRITICALLY ANALYZE CONTENT.

Many young students have learned, even before starting in elementary school, that school is about giving the right answer, the one the teacher expects. Questioning what they are told or what they see, or pushing back against it, may not be something they will naturally do in a classroom. Asking questions or offering prompts that encourage this may be a critical part of our orientation.

THE WORDING OF OUR WARM-UP PROMPTING MATTERS—ESPECIALLY WHEN IT COMES TO ENCOURAGING STUDENTS' INQUIRY.

When Jen's fourth graders get to the topic of Massive Resistance (when public schools closed in many counties rather than integrate after the

Brown v. Board of Education decision) in their study of Virginia history, *Freedom Summer*, a fabulous book by Deborah Wiles, is used for a discussion. This book, set in 1964, tells the story of two boys, one Black and one White, who are friends. A law banning segregation is passed so the town pool can be open to all. The boys are initially thrilled at this news, but when they arrive at the pool, they find that the authorities have shut it down rather than allow it to be integrated.

After the students have read the book, Jen might word the discussion's warm-up prompts like this:

"Why do you think the pool is closed?"

"If no one can use it now, that seems like a bad choice for everyone, in my mind. Why do you think anyone would make that decision?"

There are multiple discussion possibilities in *Freedom Summer*, so initial prompts that guide student focus are important; and the specific wording here gently points their attention to Massive Resistance. Despite this implicit guidance, the prompt is worded in a way that allows for individual thought. Tentative language, like "do you think" and "in my mind," make it clear that there may be different ideas, and we aren't looking for a "right" answer. We are encouraging authentic inquiry. Of course, our students may not immediately make the connections between the pool closing and schools closing that we hoped they would. Giving them some time to talk, trusting that they'll get there, with maybe a little further prompting, is crucial.

It is tempting to jump in and tell students all that we want them to know at the beginning of a tough conversation. Most ideas and concepts, however, will be more deeply and lastingly understood if we support students in constructing that knowledge themselves. The ways race impacts our society makes such ideas crucial for students to authentically understand rather than simply accept because we've told them to do so.

> It is tempting to jump in and tell students all that we want them to know at the beginning of a tough conversation.

Here's another example. In Virginia, kindergartners are expected to "recogniz[e] the [Thanksgiving] holiday and people associated with [it]" as a part of their social studies curriculum (Virginia Department of Education 2015). As many elementary teachers (especially in the early grades) are White women and have often learned and been taught using long-established educational experiences themselves, this holiday is often viewed through a very conventional lens. This typically results in five-year-olds marching around the school in black hats with white buckles or headbands with feathers in them.

Fortunately, more and more of us kindergarten and early-elementary teachers are offering their students a deeper, more meaningful exploration of Thanksgiving. When Jen teaches kindergartners and first graders, she frequently uses art and books to set them up for conversation. Leading up to Thanksgiving, she might display a print of Jean Leon Gerome Ferris's *The First Thanksgiving*, a painting that shows a long-accepted depiction of that event. Young children have strong observation skills (something we discover when we read picture books with them and they notice things in the illustrations we haven't seen, even though we've read the book dozens of times). She gives them a few days of having the print in her room before moving on to discussing it.

After they've had time to observe, unprompted, Jen shares *1621: A New Look at Thanksgiving*. This book includes many photographs of reenactments by the educators and interpreters at Plimoth Patuxet Museums. Before digging into the book, Jen shares with students that the painting they've been looking at for days and the photographs in the book were all created long after the event happened. They talk a little about what it would be like to paint or recreate for a photograph something that their grandparents or great-grandparents did as children. She asks, "Do you think it would look exactly like what they did? How would you know what to paint or create?" This prepares students to note—and eventually analyze—differences between the painting and the photographs.

As students explore the photographs in *1621: A New Look at Thanksgiving*, Jen asks them, "What do you notice is the same about these photographs and the painting? What do you notice is different?" As they note similarities and differences, she asks, "Why do you think those things are the same? Why do you think those things are different?" The specific language of these warm-up prompts provides multiple pathways for students to enter the conversation.

FIGURE 2.1
Jean Leon Gerome Ferris's *The First Thanksgiving*

WE MUST KNOW WHEN TO *MOVE ON* FROM WARM-UP PROMPTS, EVEN WHEN IT'S HARD.

It is tricky to know when to move students from engaging in a warm-up prompt to tackling the prompts that make up the real meat of the race conversation. Student-centered teachers, of course, will always (and rightfully) be tempted to be patient while students are energetically engaging a particularly interesting warm-up question—even if it wasn't meant to eat up so much time. Both Jen and Matt have often reminded teachers that "tomorrow is a thing," and that it might be a mistake to jump too quickly from a meaningful exchange. However, just as often—and we provide an example in Chapter 6—we can find ourselves mired in the warm-up prompts, trying to get our kids to say a certain thing. Perhaps the previous year, we led a great conversation that had been sparked by a delightfully insightful student response to a warm-up prompt. Now, try as we might, we can't spark the same response. Sometimes we just need to shrug and push forward to the main course.

51

"UPON FURTHER REFLECTION"
on the Prompts That Get Us Started

On the average springtime Friday afternoon, at the citywide slam poetry league that Matt runs, the typical performer approaches the microphone to the thumping bass of hip-hop and a roaring crowd of their peers and competitors. They smile nervously as they look out into the lights, maybe scan the crowd for their mentor. Once things go silent, they breathe, clear their throat, and "spit" their poem. This is how it had always gone, with little variation—until around 2012. That's when different energy entered the space. Some of the young poets started whispering "trigger warning" before they started. Then, a few weeks later, students started adding descriptors. "Trigger warning—self harm." Or "Trigger warning—abuse." For the first time, students in the audience started to stand up and exit the auditorium when they heard the phrase, wait in the hall for the poet to finish, then return. New cultural norms were developing, and they made sense to me. After all, many students from the upper-elementary grades through high school find writing about traumas to be cathartic. Some also find it liberating to share this writing before a crowd. Of course individual audience members might appreciate a warning that these topics were about to be addressed so they could either prepare themselves to hear a difficult story or decide to leave.

But it didn't take long for the norms to shift again. Instead of kids just offering trigger warnings before sharing poems about intensely personal issues, they started saying it before *any* poem that might be uncomfortable for *any*one in the audience. "Trigger warning—religion." Or "Trigger warning—police brutality." Or even "Trigger warning—racism." This was followed by a similar exodus of students—but a good look at the kids who were clogging the aisles showed that leaving itself had become a show within the show. Students were looking around, whispering to each other, "I'm out. We should be out, right?" *Staying*, it seemed, opened one up to criticism. *Leaving* meant that you had the requisite sensitivity. This bothered me. Especially as I saw our youngest audience members, both those from our elementary school teams and the younger siblings of my high school students, watching the spectacle. What had started as a simple and fair warning to fellow students had morphed into something much less authentic. Also, it was a *poetry slam*. In a poetry slam, people share ideas—some of them are heavy, some of them are irreverent, some of them are even profane (although Matt doesn't allow profanity across the board—it is a youth event, after all!). When one goes to a poetry slam, one should know what to expect.

To some degree, when a student enters a race discussion, they (and their families) should know what to expect. They will be loved, listened to, and, to a developmentally appropriate degree, *challenged*. We must prepare students for conversations with this "trigger warning" era's best intentions—allowing our students the space and opportunity to protect themselves from unnecessary trauma—and *not* with the era's worst consequences—encouraging performative sensitivity and avoidance of tough issues.

Prompts that get us out of race conversations

It also matters which prompts we use to exit race conversations. We need to make sure students *leave* each of the myriad interactions in a race conversation—both exchanges with us and exchanges with their peers—with a clear idea of what has just happened. Parents of young children might be especially familiar with the importance of classroom interactions that end well. All of our children have shared with us that they've had a "great!" or "horrible!" day in this or that class but then had trouble explaining what had sparked this sentiment. *A lot* happens in a student's average day, and much of it threatens to dilute and/or warp their memory of any one class conversation, regardless of its momentary impact. Without careful attention to the way interactions end, the play-by-play that makes it home, or that sticks with students, might bear little relationship to what actually happened in the class discussion.

This requires us, as the facilitators of the conversation, to be fully present, actively processing the conversation as it is happening. It is important for us to consider how we will *exit* the conversation even while in the midst of it, even while students share their thinking and respond to each other's thinking.

To prepare for a successful exit, it's helpful to offer summaries of what has been said at key intervals. Summarizing *as we go along*—and not waiting for the end—not only helps to keep students engaged (by helping them hold on to the thread), but it also helps the conversation's ending feel less abrupt. We might jump in and say, "It sounds like I'm hearing Fatmata say _____, and Alicia agreed and added _____. D'Angelo seemed a bit less certain and asked about _____. What are you all thinking now?" Summarizing in that way values students' ideas and keeps the conversation moving on track, as we focus on student comments that push the conversation forward.

Eventually, we will get to the exit point that we've been building to. If you've spent much time with very young children, you have seen the power of what comes last, how what is most recent sticks with students most strongly. Jen's oldest child called computers "puters" as a toddler because the final sounds of a long word were what she could hold on to. Our brains can't retain everything, and the newer information and ideas remain more vivid, in general. That makes the final (at least for the moment) summary of a race conversation crucially important to help students come away with ideas that are as unambiguous as possible about the conversation.

A SUMMARY AT THE END OF A CONVERSATION ALSO ALLOWS US TO DO SEVERAL IMPORTANT THINGS:

1. It brings together ideas that came up throughout the conversation but may not have been as clearly connected as we would have liked. Sometimes this happens because the ideas pop up at different times throughout the conversation, and we want to be sure the students notice the connections. Other times it can happen because the focus of the conversation went a different way, and students

might have missed an important connection. A summary allows us to reinforce connections that might otherwise have slipped past.

2. It reminds students of what was said and asked and why those things are important. The recap could sound like this: "There were so many thoughts and questions today about Thanksgiving and what we know about that history and how we know it. You all explored ideas about who told the stories that we heard and who didn't tell stories. That makes a big difference in our understanding because not everyone sees things the same way. You asked some great questions about how European settlers and the indigenous people might have helped each other and why. You are recognizing that there is a lot about history that we think we know but that, maybe, we don't know as much as we think we do." The summary is the chance to tie up the ends as much as we can.

3. It provides a sense of closure. Not every conversation will end with full closure, but we want to offer our students some sense of satisfaction and not send them away unsettled or confused if we can avoid it. That might mean our closure is more about stating some uncertainties aloud to reassure students that we don't have all the answers all the time and it is okay that they don't either. We might say, "There were a lot of ideas and questions that came up in our conversation today. I have lots of new things to think about. I also still have some things I want to learn more about, which is really exciting. The learning never stops!"

Summarizing at the end of the conversation is a task that might be carefully shared with kids. Once students, especially in upper elementary, have seen us model good habits, like listening carefully, grabbing the big ideas to write down, and asking students to repeat something when we need them to, they might be encouraged to give summarizing a try themselves. The goal in the recap is to bring the *main* points of the discussion back to the top of the students' minds. Sometimes these important ideas came up early in the race conversation. If that's the case, the summary will bring them back to the forefront of our minds as we move on.

"UPON FURTHER REFLECTION"
on the Prompts That Wrap Things Up

Right as *Not Light* hit its final stages of postproduction in 2018, Matt read Daniel Kahneman's bestselling *Thinking, Fast and Slow* (2011). And for the first of many times in the years since, he wished he could add *just one more page* to the book. While teaching about his *Peak/End Theory*, which argues that we best remember a moment's emotional peak and how it ends, Kahneman describes a fascinating experiment that illustrates the psychological importance of ending moments well. In short, participants were asked to submerge their hands in painfully cold water for sixty seconds. After a recovery period, they were asked to do it again. This second time however, the experimenter opened a secret valve that let slightly warmer water into the tank. Not enough to make it not hurt, but enough to make it slightly less painful. This second dip lasted ninety seconds. The participants were then asked which of the two experiences they'd prefer to repeat. The *only* logical answer is the first, which involved less time spent in pain. But 80 percent of participants chose the second! They remembered this experience being less painful because it *ended* less painfully. This experiment can speak to everything from uncomfortable medical procedures (make sure the last few minutes are less painful than the middle) to vacation planning (to feel refreshed, do the rigorous backpacking at the top of the trip and *end* with the beach relaxation) (Kahneman 2011).

The "cold hands" experiment illustrates the importance of *ending* both sensitive personal interactions and larger, complex group exchanges well. Even if the learning was uncomfortable, as the learning in race conversations can sometimes be, we can not only shift the energy but also impact how the entire moment is ultimately remembered. Ending prompts that are deliberately positive, encouraging, or reassuring can be the reason a meaningful race conversation retains its power.

WHAT DID THAT KID JUST SAY? WHAT ON EARTH DO I DO *NOW*?

During the all-important minutes between our *entrance* into the conversation and our *exit* out of it, we make hundreds of decisions. Oddly enough, the more student-driven the conversation, the more real-time decisions *we*, as teachers, have to make: Which words should we emphasize when offering a prompt? How much "wait time" is necessary for students to process it? Which emphatically raised waving hand do we call on? The more we get to know our students, the simpler *some* of these decisions become. Yet, one real-time communication decision bedevils rookie teachers as much as it continually humbles veterans—*What do we do when a kid says something that seems unrelated to our planned thread of conversation?* Do we respond to this non sequitur with *flexibility* or *agility*?

First, two quick definitions:

1. We show *flexibility* when we *bend* the conversation back toward the ideas we intended to explore.

2. We use *agility* when we *table* the anticipated thread (temporarily or permanently) and reprompt the class from the student's comment.

Discerning which "non sequiturs" require flexibility and which require agility has higher stakes than we might think, and our execution of either technique often impacts students' willingness to contribute to future race conversations.

Young children, whose lives have, so far, been shorter than ours have been, often make connections that feel, to us at least, like a stretch. Typically, our first instinct is to steer conversations back "on track" from students' seemingly tangential ideas. It is a default choice probably because it's seemingly the safest one. We are less likely to get into trouble if we stick to our planned discussion thread. Students are probably less likely to hurt each other, too. While understandable, this instinct can keep our class conversations from reaching their truest potential. When our students share fresh ideas, the ones that seem to come from nowhere, they are often stepping out onto a ledge. As confident as they might seem on

57

the surface, it takes vulnerability to say, "This reminds me of _____!" when they aren't sure that *anyone else* will find their observation either interesting or important. If our redirections from contributions like these are curt or dismissive, students are more likely to question the value of sharing ideas that pop into their heads.

It can be helpful to think of some standard language we might use to smoothly get conversations back on track from students' random connections—while not squashing their instinct to share. Although this language may not be necessary every day, *not* having it and then trying to craft a meaningful redirect in the midst of a sea of ten-year-olds waving their hands can be a bit awkward. The moment can be more comfortable for all if we have prepared for the possibility.

The following text box shows some redirections that Jen uses. As you read them, notice how none of her responses send the message that the students' comments were *useless* to the current discussion. All of them, in fact, acknowledge that there might be a meaningful connection—one that the class might even explore further on the way to the goals of the conversation. In other words, the precise wording of these redirections makes Jen's flexibility clear.

SOME POSSIBLE LANGUAGE FOR REDIRECTING STUDENTS

> "That's an interesting point. We will try to get back to it after we discuss the idea at hand."

> "Thank you for that idea. Can you help us see how that's connected to what we were discussing?"

> "You have a lot of thoughts about this topic. Let's see what others think about the idea we were talking about and then get to new ideas."

> "Your classmates look interested in that question. Let's write it down so we can come back to it when we wrap up this thought."

Of course, other students may have already taken in their classmate's tangential comment and begun to connect with and consider it. Our reorienting statement may need to be repeated to be effective. Or we might be surprised when a student—the one who made the comment or one of their classmates—solidly connects the tangent with the topic under discussion.

THE TIME FOR *AGILITY* IN RACE CONVERSATIONS WITH ELEMENTARY STUDENTS

Jen often jokes that it takes half a year before she knows her new kiddos well enough to navigate moments when students offer up tangents. (She doesn't think it *really* takes that long, but it definitely takes a while.) As a result, at the start of the school year she is far more likely to steer a conversation back to the original track rather than follow a student's seemingly out-of-nowhere lead. It isn't until she has had the chance to listen to her elementary students talk, both formally in class and informally with her and each other, that she feels confident in her ability to identify when a student's seemingly random comment might present a productive new path rather than an unproductive dead end.

These times are tricky and require a bit of bravery on the part of the teacher. While flexibility might come more naturally for most teachers, agility is often a leap. It requires that we *trust our students to be able to follow a complex discussion when it quickly takes a new direction. (And sometimes to lead it there.)*

Here's a quick example. On Constitution Day, Jen told her third graders that on that day in 1787, thirty-nine men had signed the United States Constitution, which is the basis for the country's laws. She meant for students to notice that only White men had signed it and discuss why that might be. She showed them a picture of those men, and they indeed noted that all of them were White. Check. She then gave them a bit more context by telling them that they were also all landowners and relatively wealthy. It was at this point that a few students noticed a familiar face among the signers of the Constitution. "Hey! That's George Washington!" They immediately started sharing random "facts" they'd learned about him ("Did you know he had *wooden teeth*?"). The celebrity sighting was all of a sudden hogging her students' focus.

As Jen considered what to do, repeated comments about the founding father's wooden teeth gave her inspiration. She first decided to gently correct the myth, explaining that his dentures were made, at least in part, from *human* teeth. Her third graders mulled this over and thought about how on earth that could have happened. It didn't take long for them to naturally get to Washington's ownership of enslaved people, and from there to the likelihood that teeth taken from enslaved people had been used to make his dentures. This wasn't where Jen had meant to take them, but it was nonetheless a worthwhile journey.

Agility is a complex skill that is developed with increased experience and practice. That said, there's never likely to be a time when agility is completely free of worry or hesitation. However, the better we know our students (especially after the activities described in Chapter 1) and the more deeply we know the topic we're discussing, the more likely it is that we will be able to be agile in ways that support our young students' curiosity . . . and pivot back in the inevitable moments when our agility leads a good conversation to a dead end.

POP-UP CONVERSATIONS

When a big racial event "goes down" in the world (a big trial verdict, a series of protests, an insurrection), teachers face a special dilemma. The next day, do we "table" our planned curriculum and lead a class conversation about it? Or do we keep pushing forward with our previous plans? When something troublesome has happened on a more local level—in either the school or the community—do we talk about it immediately with the kids? What if we just get a great idea at 2:00 a.m., or during our drive into work? Should we kick it off while there's still fire in our bellies? Or should we wait?

In *Not Light*, Matt defined such unplanned (or lightly planned) discussions as "pop-up" conversations. More than anything else, they are a reaction to a moment in time. And they make both of us *very* nervous. Anecdotally, it seems that most of the biggest mistakes in race conversations happen during pop-up conversations. And we humbly think it's hard to dispute the reasoning *Not Light* gives for our nervousness:

The lack of discussion planning leaves me too many blind spots. I've not checked and rechecked the wording of my prompts for implicit or explicit bias. I've not anticipated possible conflicts between students. I've not gathered up sources to contextualize various points that might be made. Essentially, I am flying blind. I've heard that when rookie pilots fly into a cloud, they can get so confused that they don't trust their instruments. In such cases they've been known to fly out of clouds completely upside down. Or worse, they instinctively keep climbing to avoid hitting the ground, which causes their plane to stall out—then crash. When a conversation crashes, teachers waste important capital with students. Or end up in the newspapers.

(Kay 2018, 242)

For this reason, we believe that *most* pop-up conversations are best folded into planned curriculum—using some of the suggestions that we are about to share in both Chapter 3 and the stories that will make up Part 2 of this book. However, sometimes—not *nearly* as often as the world would have us think—the racial moment is big enough that it's only right to drop everything and discuss it with our students. Here, Jen will offer some tips for how to handle these moments.

Pop-up conversations in the elementary classroom

It is usually easier for us who teach in elementary schools to avoid pop-up conversations than it is for our secondary school counterparts. Most of our students are less aware, in general, of all that is going on in the world than their middle and high school neighbors. They are not clueless, by any stretch of the imagination, but they are less likely to be passionately engaged with big news items. That makes it even more critical that we be thoughtful about when we lead pop-up race conversations, as our students are often unlikely to have enough background knowledge to participate.

So how do we know when to engage?

The election of 2016, about which Matt wrote in *Not Light*, was definitely one of those moments for Jen's third graders. For several weeks, her students, many of them first- or second-generation immigrant students from El Salvador and Honduras, had been talking among themselves and to her about the upcoming election. One third grader had approached her privately to discuss what might happen to both her and her younger brother if Donald Trump were elected and her parents deported (not in quite that language but clearly with that meaning). So after the election, Jen knew they could not ignore it and simply go about their regular routine.

When they sat down together for Morning Meeting on the day after the election, she decided to give students the opportunity to talk, if they so desired. Jen said, "Before we get started with our day, is there anything anyone wants to talk about?"

> Jen felt that the timing was right because she knew the election was *already* on her students' minds.

The students sat there quietly for a moment before one boy said, incredulously, "Trump won." The floodgates opened. Students had thoughts to share and questions to ask. It was clear that many families had talked about the election results at home that morning. It was a rare moment in which all, or close enough to all, of her third graders were aware of—and knowledgeable about—a high-stakes current event that had nothing to do with their curriculum. As Spanish-speaking young people with strong connections to other countries, her students had felt attacked, misunderstood, and unvalued throughout the election and were now hurt, scared, and angry at the result. Jen felt that the timing was right because she knew the election was *already* on her students' minds. Knowing that a high enough percentage of the class is generally aware of an issue is a baseline factor when deciding if a whole-class pop-up conversation is worth the risk. (Remember, some families may have worked hard to keep their children from hearing news that they believed their children were too young to hear. If we are then going to engage these issues, it *cannot* be without proper planning.)

Sometimes, educators might assume that because an issue has had a high profile, it warrants a pop-up conversation. In 2017, when the mass shooting happened at the concert in Las Vegas, Jen's principal reached out to all of the staff about students who might be feeling some anxiety or fear. Jen spent a few days listening carefully, watching closely, to see if any of her students showed signs of being impacted by that shooting. Jen never saw a thing, and no student mentioned it. She didn't force the issue.

At about that same time, however, Immigration and Customs Enforcement (ICE) was conducting raids in nearby neighborhoods with many immigrant residents. That was something about which some of Jen's students were feeling anxiety. From what she could tell, not *all* of her students were aware or worried, so she opted not to have a whole-class conversation about it. However, Jen spoke with individual students as she observed their reactions and gave them opportunities to speak with a school counselor. Because some of them felt so personally threatened by these raids, she did not want to spread the fear to students who were not feeling it yet by bringing the topic up with the whole class.

There should always be a compelling, time-sensitive reason to engage the whole class in a pop-up conversation about race. (If there isn't an urgent reason to talk about it *right now*, remember that it doesn't mean we never talk about it; it just means that we should fold the topic into a powerful, well-planned conversation.) This compelling, time-sensitive reason might be students' personal connection to an issue, as with the 2016 presidential election (about which many of Jen's Spanish-speaking students had an emotional connection) or the ICE raids—if more students had shown an awareness of them.

Sometimes a conversation checks both of the boxes we've mentioned— enough students know about it, and their concern makes it urgent—but our privileges can cause us to still mishandle it. Jen teaches in the suburbs of Washington, DC, and the events of 9/11 triggered strong reactions across the community. Teachers were directed, on that day, to say nothing to their students about what was happening. On September 12, the schools were closed for reasons of safety, since it was not known what else might be happening just down the road at the Pentagon or the White House. When Jen's fourth graders returned to school on September 13, they had *many* strong emotions. Jen had spent a lot of time thinking about how to help them process and cope with what had happened. What she, as a young teacher, had not prepared for was having a Sikh student say during their Morning Meeting, "My people did this." Jen *had* prepared to address their fears and their grief and their anger. However, she had not considered discussing the attacks through the lens of race or religion. And, in that moment, this unpreparedness showed. She stammered out a response, an attempt to assuage his guilt and let him know that he, and "his people," were not to blame.

Jen knows now that she should have been prepared for this specific angle. The racist and xenophobic nature of many people's responses to 9/11 was very clear. And yet, she had not considered that her young students would be aware of the racism, or would actually experience it themselves. This was a faulty assumption. So while this was a topic that (a) many of her students were aware of and (b) sparked emotions that it was urgent to support them through, her own fear and privilege kept her from being the teacher to lead the discussion well.

In the twenty years since that moment, Jen has learned a lot (and a lot of it the hard way) about both when to lead pop-up conversations and how to make sure that her privileges and fears are less in the way of success. She suggests we all do a few things:

1. We have to increase our general awareness of what issues might be impacting our students. For Jen, that means listening to NPR on her daily commute and subscribing to a daily newspaper. She knows she will still miss plenty, but she has built routines into her daily life that help her know what is happening locally, nationally, and globally that may impact her students and their families.

2. We have to listen to our students when we're *not* actively teaching them. This is helped by the house talk activities described in Chapter 1, but it extends to informal moments: when students first arrive in our classroom, when we're transitioning between activities or locations, at recess, and so on. Each of these moments is a micro-opportunity to strengthen our awareness of what's going on in students' lives. This allows us to prepare, at least somewhat, for more personal connections that students might bring up seemingly out of the blue.

3. We also have to listen to our students when we *are* actively teaching them. It's easy to use certain moments during lessons, like when students are speaking to each other in small groups,

to tune out for a second or plan ahead. However, making the effort to actually plug into their conversations with classmates gives us insight into what is weighing on their minds and hearts, and very practically lets us know which world or community issues they might be aware of.

4. We have to pay attention to their behaviors in quiet moments. By watching students at these times, such as when they arrive and when they leave for the day, we might see clues about how they're doing, and what they might be likely to bring up with little to no prompting.

And for those occasions when, considering all of this, we have decided that a pop-up conversation is necessary, Matt provided guidelines in *Not Light* about how to make sure we lead it well.

1. During pop-up conversations, we provide space for vulnerability. We do not *demand* it. The real-time issues that inspire pop-up conversations are often the same ones that benefit most from the house talk relationships mentioned in Chapter 1. We should never assume that an individual student wants to "open up" among classmates—and teachers—who do not share their racial or cultural background. Nor should we assume that because *one* student does, others from a similar background will. Like many other interactions, pop-up conversations require us to meet each individual student where they are.

2. While providing this space, we take the time to explicitly reestablish the listening protocols from Chapter 1. The intensity of the moment might lead students to forget (or not care) that these ground rules still apply.

3. The warm-up prompts take on a special importance. We must own that we are about to have a pop-up conversation and explain to students why we thought it was important enough to have in place of the lesson that they were expecting.

4. Even while we might not always be able to lead students to "closure," we need to give them space to get to some clarity or

draw important conclusions. If that means the conversation stretches into the next day, so be it. (This is especially important given some of our youngest students' attention spans. As we know, we can only stay with one conversation for so long before they get antsy.) It's also important that we openly communicate this intention to follow up.

As teachers, we have many choices to make when we guide conversations, especially about race. Those choices can make a significant difference in the success of such conversations.

A NOTE ON LANGUAGE

Young children are less likely than older students to be aware of the myriad meanings words and phrases might currently have. They also might quickly adopt the language they hear us using. As a result, we must be deliberate about the language choices we make in our prompts and thoughtful about our own contributions to class conversations. This is especially true in the heat of pop-up conversations, which, by definition, happen in situations that are unplanned. How we speak in these spontaneous moments about people's identities is likely to influence our students' own language choices.

Language also evolves, with appropriate terms for races, ethnicities, genders, classes, abilities, linguistic groups, and religions being updated frequently. This is daunting to consider, and we are likely (even guaranteed) to make mistakes. That shouldn't stop us from paying close attention to the best current terminology, then making the effort to be as inclusive and respectful as we can with our language. We do this because it is the right thing to do, and also because our language will always be a model for our students.

CHAPTER 3

IMPROVING OUR DIALOGIC PEDAGOGY

This chapter will dive into the nitty-gritty of how to design and execute powerful race conversations. But first, it's worth it to ask the obvious question.

WHY ARE WE *REALLY* DOING THIS?

Maybe we do it because we *have* to. Our school might have just launched an equity initiative and handed us a fresh curriculum that doesn't center White voices. Community members might have advocated for curriculum changes and won. Maybe the content itself (the sixties-era Civil Rights Movement, for example) forces us to lead at least a basic version of the conversation. It might be easy to criticize others' (or feel shame about our own) "I have to" motivations. But this is unfair. After all, many of us *started* doing something worthwhile only because someone made us try.

Or maybe we do it because we *want* to. We might want to assuage a sense of personal guilt. We might want to be cool. We might want to acknowledge (and shoo away) an "elephant" in our classroom. Maybe talking to our students about race gives us joy. These "I want to" motivations can push our class conversations to the mountaintop just as often as they nudge them off of a cliff. For example, perhaps the high-profile race stories of the past few years have inspired us to confront certain race, color, or class privileges. This might inspire us to lead the upcoming race conversation with humility (mountaintop), or they might make us feel like we've got to "solve" racism in one moment (cliff).

There is an unfortunate link between most "I have to" motivations and most "I want to" motivations: they don't (at least, authentically) motivate *kids*. Young students, for instance, don't instinctively care that their teacher is now accountable for teaching a certain book or time period a certain way. They likewise don't care about their teacher's racial guilt, nor are they invested in an adult's desire to be cool. If we want kids to consistently buy in, we must consistently give them reasons to do so.

SO HOW DO WE MAKE RACE CONVERSATIONS ABOUT *THEM*?

The following two propositions help us keep kids at the forefront of our race conversations. Both require listening closely to our students, during both formal class discussions and informal interactions.

1. We can plan future race conversations based on student interests and questions.

During class conversations about race, students are likely to become passionate about certain ideas or, at a minimum, more curious about and interested in them. Sometimes this interest or passion may be exactly what we expected and, guided by a little real-time flexibility on our end, might fuel a powerful conversation that pretty much goes where we were planning to go. Sometimes, it's not what we expected, and we face a real-time choice to show agility, making authentic student interest the core of the rest of the conversation.

When we introduced agility in the last chapter, we meant to highlight it as a teacher communication skill that can benefit a single day's discussion. However, our willingness to let race conversations take a fresh direction based on our students' interests can be bigger than one moment.

One of the books Jen uses frequently is Sandra Neil Wallace's, *Between the Lines: How Ernie Barnes Went from the Football Field to the Art Gallery*, because it draws in students interested in sports and students interested in art and students interested in history. This appeal to many different interests allows a variety of questions to arise and intersect in cool ways. It is also a way to get young learners thinking about how race has impacted professional desires and plans across many types of careers. As a child, Ernie Barnes loved to draw, but, in North Carolina in the 1940s, he could not see a professional path forward in art as a Black man. Barnes was also a skilled football player and was offered scholarships by many universities to play. After college, he went on to play in the NFL for several years before an injury ended his career. He then returned to

> If we want kids to consistently buy in, we must consistently give them reasons to do so.

his first love and became a salaried artist for the NFL. Barnes was eventually able to make a career in a way he had not been able to envision as a child. That option, crucially, was not widely available. Students can have interesting conversations about the barriers in Barnes's way and what, ultimately, allowed him to overcome them.

In those conversations, Jen often finds students who are drawn to Barnes's time in the NFL and interested in the role race played in that experience. (Barnes was originally drafted by the Redskins, but they traded him immediately upon learning that he was Black. The Redskins (now the Commanders) did not integrate their team until 1962, and were the last NFL franchise to do so.) This student interest often leads to discussions about the role that race plays in various sports. Other students are intrigued by Barnes's art. Over the next few days, they explore and discuss Barnes's influences, and how he used sports and race as important themes in his work. This then leads to analyzing and appreciating other artists through the same lens. Listening closely and following our students' interests and questions are powerful ways to ensure that *they* are the driving force behind many meaningful race conversations.

2. We can support our students in sharing with wider audiences.

Encouraging students to share with audiences beyond their teacher and classmates, and offering them avenues to do so, is a powerful way to ensure that the learning is about them. Sharing with wider audiences is not something that happens frequently in many elementary classrooms. One result of this is that, as researchers have observed, "by the end of elementary school, students seldom write unless they have to and then only because it 'counts'" (Calfee and Miller 2007, 266). We can help students see their learning about race as meaningful and valued by offering them ways to share it with a wider audience. There are a number of possibilities for this.

- Students can work with some classmates to record a podcast.

- Students can post writing on a class blog.

- Students can create posters to display at school.

- Students can join the school's morning news show as a guest to share their learning.

Some options, obviously, have gatekeepers. In order to hang posters or share on the morning news show, students will likely need permission from an adult in the school. In many schools, some of these opportunities might not exist, or if they do, students may not even realize it. Our students' age and level of experience sharing with a wider audience will determine how much help they need from us. They may need us to help them secure permission and prepare for their presentations.

Of course, we can offer sharing opportunities that do not have outside gatekeepers. We might set up a class blog where students can write at any time. Or we can make it so that their posts need to be approved before they are published. Again, we can determine what is the best fit for our students depending on their age and experience. The same goes for recording a podcast or other options for recording themselves. Audio recording, in whatever form, is a fabulous option for early-elementary students who are not yet ready to write all of their ideas. Sharing these recordings may be a bit more complicated, but offering students the option to record their new thinking and new understandings is a place to start showing them that it is about them. (We can post these recordings to a class blog or video website.)

Conversations about race are likely to result in new passions, questions, and ideas. Listening closely to our students and following their lead, as much as possible, will support their ongoing learning and ensure that *they* are at the front of our work.

SO WHAT KIND OF CLASS CONVERSATIONS EXIST? AND WHICH ARE BEST FOR RACE CONVERSATIONS?

Matt coaches both varsity basketball and football and is a generally rabid sports fan. One of the lessons of coaching is that certain plays tend to complement each other. Across many sports, one play lays the groundwork for a future play's success, and these complementary plays are usually organized into easily definable groups, or "packages." Despite the endless list of *possible* ways to coach each sport, most coaches have only a few "packages" that they feel truly comfortable with—and few stray from them when deciding what to teach their athletes.

In *Not Light*, Matt pointed out the similarities between these coaching decisions and how we plan and execute our class discussions. He separated classroom conversations into three buckets, *Whole Class*, *Small Learning Community*, and *One on One*. (Had the book come out in 2020, he *certainly* would have added *Online*. We will here.) Each of these buckets holds countless discussion activities, but you—like a good coach—should pick the ones that work best with your students, the ideas in your curriculum, and your natural talents and personality, and then put them in heavy rotation. It's better to do a few things well than to do a lot of things poorly.

Ultimately, it's not about finding any one magic race-talk activity. It's about the following four principles:

1. **Never rely on one bucket to get the whole job done.** Sometimes, we only feel comfortable having the kids in a whole-class format. Or perhaps we sit them in groups, and *all* conversation happens in groups. This lack of variety results in missed opportunities for different kinds of learners.

2. **Never "silo" what works.** Sometimes the kids find a conversational activity incredibly powerful, but instead of finding ways to bring it back, we pack it away in mothballs for next year. We attach good techniques to a single subject, or unit, or lesson, instead of thinking of them as flat-out good pedagogy that needs to get in wherever it fits.

3. **Remember to show how activities complement each other.** Sometimes we see connections between conversational techniques that our students don't see. It's best to point out these links and not assume that students see them.

4. **Make structural *and* race-specific reflection a habit, especially *after* important conversations.** In the next few pages, we will describe some of the specific post-conversation reflections that we've found to be most useful, as well as practical advice for the activities in each bucket.

Whole-Class-Conversation Reflection Questions

ISSUE: Supporting "introverts" and "extroverts" in whole-class conversations	
GENERAL QUESTIONS	RACE-SPECIFIC QUESTIONS
1. What behaviors have led me to think that a student is shy? **2.** How am I making sure I am holding space for more introverted students in whole-class conversations? **3.** Do I have a systematic method for assessing how well students are listening to each other?	**1.** Do I recognize that there are different cultural elements that impact how often students may speak in class? How are my discussion plans responsive to this? **2.** Are students who are unwilling to speak in whole-class conversations actually shy? Or is it that they do not feel safe engaging this specific race topic publicly in my class? **3.** Are "participation points" or other would-be incentives having the intended impact? What is my method for finding out? Are there race-specific consequences to these incentives?

Jen's Suggestions: Whole-class conversations, at any age, will have some individuals who remain quiet and some who speak quite frequently. We might be tempted to require, as so many online courses do, that each student share once or twice. Conversely, we might allow each student to speak only a limited number of times. The downside to these strategies is that they artificially control the conversation. (For example, let's say we have an "everyone speaks twice" rule—but a student only has one quality point to make that day. The next day, however, they have three. The rule encourages them to overtalk on day one, while artificially restricting them on day two.) Students who might dominate the conversation are better served by learning to control their voices (as explained in Chapter One) than by having their comments arbitrarily restricted.

We need to also remind ourselves that *listening* in whole-class conversations is as valuable as *speaking* in whole-class conversations. When our first graders are nodding along as a classmate shares, or our fourth graders are making the connection sign with their hands, they are just as active in the whole-class conversation as the speakers they are listening to. (Later in this chapter we'll explore ways to assess students' understanding of a conversation, which can feel extra important for those students who tend to be quieter.)

Additional Whole-Class-Conversation Reflection Questions

ISSUE: Managing my talk-time as a teacher in whole-class conversations	
GENERAL QUESTIONS	**RACE-SPECIFIC QUESTIONS**
1. Am I fully understanding the weight of my voice in this conversation? What are the implications of this authority? **2.** How am I communicating that it is acceptable to disagree publicly with any of my statements? Have I shown students how to do so both respectfully and with academic rigor?	**1.** In what ways might I unintentionally be centering my own lived and cultural experiences in this conversation?

Jen's Suggestions: Personally, this is one of both Jen's and Matt's greatest challenges. We both love to talk. Yet, controlling our voices is important because we are, by default, the authority in our classrooms.

Anything we say is going to carry a lot of weight. As hard as we may work to ensure that our students see each other as resources for learning, we will always have an exalted position as the adult in the room.

The questions above are ones we must ask ourselves regularly. We must be ever mindful of how much weight our students—especially our youngest—will give anything we say. While our students can say things without pausing to think (although we might prefer they did pause!), we don't have that luxury. If, in a race conversation, we make a statement that unintentionally centers our own experiences, something that is very easy to do when we have rushed our discussion planning, we need to give ourselves space and time in the moment to recenter our students.

Small-Group-Conversation Reflection Questions

ISSUE: Ensuring small-group conversations remain on track and appropriate when the teacher is not immediately able to hear everything that is said	
GENERAL QUESTIONS	RACE-SPECIFIC QUESTIONS
1. How might I keep students' conversational focus on the subject at hand if I am not hovering?	**1.** I may not be aware of racial misconceptions shared by students during small-group race conversations. How might I anticipate these misconceptions and adjust my warm-ups to make them less likely? How might I remedy the situation when I fail at this?
	2. I may not be aware of improper language that is used in small-group race conversations. Are students comfortable sharing with me when something a classmate has said makes them feel unsafe?

Jen's Suggestions: Small-group race conversations can cause us anxiety. With upper-elementary students we might worry that conversations will go off topic and become inappropriate. With younger elementary students we might worry that conversations will go off topic and get goofy. With any age group, we might be concerned that students will say things that are, purposely or not, hurtful to their classmates. There's a lot of trust involved in holding small-group conversations.

It's important that our students are able to share with us when small-group conversations go awry. Some students will likely feel comfortable coming to us and saying there was a problem and explaining their concerns. Others may not. We need to consider what strategies we can put into place to offer students ways to approach us.

We might, for instance, develop a hand or written symbol for our youngest students, a way they can silently let us know they want to talk to us about a conversation. They might draw a sad face or a *T* for "talk" on a paper to give us. Or they might make a *T* in American Sign Language (make a fist with their thumb between their first two fingers) to signal us. That could let us know to check in with them to learn what happened. Older students could write a quick note to us (or use the previously mentioned symbols, as those don't have to be limited to young students) so that we touch base with them. If students know they have some way to address concerns about a conversation, they are more likely to feel more comfortable and confident participating in it.

Additional Small-Group-Conversation Reflection Questions

ISSUE: Taking advantage of greater intimacy in small-group conversations	
GENERAL QUESTIONS	**RACE-SPECIFIC QUESTIONS**
1. How do I best group the students for a small-group conversation? Put friends together? Split up students who talk a lot? Group them by academic achievement levels?	**1.** Would this particular conversation benefit from racial or ethnic affinity groups? **2.** How have I encouraged students to take advantage of the more intimate setting to ask questions they feel more self-conscious about?

Jen's Suggestions: There is no one right way to form a small discussion group. It all depends on the dynamics that you see developing among your students, the time of year, and the goals for the discussion. Earlier in the school year we might lean more toward allowing students to form their own small groups. Choosing their conversation mates might make it less intimidating to engage in a meaningful conversation. As our community grows, we might want to group together students who speak less frequently, as it is possible they will feel more comfortable speaking if they don't have classmates constantly talking and there is some silence they can speak into.

After small-group conversations, we can solicit feedback from our students to gain some insight into how well our groupings worked. We might do something as simple as asking students how they felt their conversation went, on a scale of one to five. They can hold up fingers or write a number on a slip of paper. We can also have a quick survey ready, with just a few questions, such as "How comfortable did you feel participating in today's conversation?" They can respond on a scale of one to five or by circling an emoji, ranging from a sad face to a smiley face. Getting some sense of our students' experiences in the conversation will help us make groups in the future.

One-on-One-Conversation Reflection Questions

ISSUE: Effectively setting up one-on-one situations, in which there's too much going on for the teacher to direct specific conversations	
GENERAL QUESTIONS	RACE-SPECIFIC QUESTIONS
1. How can I incentivize my students to stay with the discussion prompt? 2. How do I best pair the students for a conversation? 3. With one-on-one discussion activities, students are tasked with either speaking or listening. This leaves no "rest time." With this in mind, what's the ideal length for these discussion activities?	1. Some students will be more eager to ask questions in one-on-one situations than they are in forums that have a built-in audience. These questions might put students of color in awkward situations. How can I best support them?

Jen's Suggestions: Elementary students tend to love one-on-one conversations because every voice has an opportunity to be heard. It may be only the one classmate who hears what they have to say, but they don't have to wait, hold it in, and maybe not get to share it at all. Tell elementary students, be they kindergartners or fifth graders, "Turn and talk with a partner," and we immediately see them scoot to a classmate and get going.

Just as with small-group conversations, sometimes we may want to allow students to find their own partner (often that is the quickest option), and sometimes we may have reasons to partner students up deliberately. We may want our students to talk with someone whose life experiences are likely to be different and who will bring a different perspective to the conversation. Other times we may want students to talk with someone who is likely to share an understanding and bring a level of connection to the conversation.

One-on-one conversations tend to be our quickest conversations. We don't need as much time for two voices as we do when there are more. Keeping these conversations shorter can allow for more opportunities to turn and talk again or to share with the whole class. That said, we certainly don't want to rush these conversations. In many elementary classrooms, we can gently lean in to eavesdrop on conversations while keeping an ear open for when the buzz begins to slow. When partner conversations come to a natural end, students typically pause a bit. If we wait too long, they'll start a new (likely off-topic) conversation! But if we listen for that natural pause, we know when to bring students back. One strategy to try and ease that tension is to bring students back to the whole group by counting backward. Start at ten or five or three, depending on how long you think they'll need, and count down to zero. As you count, students have the opportunity to wrap up their talk, to come to some kind of conclusion before having to stop. Of course, we may not always want to wait long enough for that natural pause. If it doesn't come (or we fear we might have missed it), we can return students to the whole group when we feel they've had a chance to dig into the question at hand, even if they might want to dig even more. We must communicate that our stopping a one-on-one conversation doesn't mean we're stopping *all* talk on a topic. Another chance will be coming.

Online-Conversation Reflection Questions

ISSUE: Keeping everyone feeling connected and safe	
GENERAL QUESTIONS	RACE-SPECIFIC QUESTIONS
1. How can I take advantage of the additional modalities to keep kids connected (chat windows, breakout rooms, quick polls, etc.)? **2.** Without access to their body language, how can I check in to see how connected students are to the discourse?	**1.** A classroom is mostly secure. We know who is in the room all the time. When we are virtual, we no longer have any control over who is listening to the conversation. How do we ensure that kids feel safe contributing to a race conversation in these circumstances?

Jen's Suggestions: We all learned the benefits and challenges of online schooling in recent years. (Jen personally was a big fan of being able to do laundry during lunch time.) For educators who value student conversations, online school was a big hill to climb. Keeping students engaged and determining how well conversations were going was tough, especially small-group or partner conversations in breakout rooms.

The chat is a surprisingly useful tool for allowing voices to be heard (at least in those grades in which students can type meaningfully) and making it possible for students to subtly reach out to us when there are problems. Just as we can encourage students to let us know when there is a problem in the physical classroom, we can do the same in a virtual setting. Younger students can use a predetermined emoji to let us know they want to talk with us about a concern. A quick poll after any conversation can also offer us some feedback to help for future planning.

PROMPTING, REVISITED

Throughout Chapter 2, we talked about the sort of prompts we use to enter and exit race conversations. We argued, essentially, that a race conversation's appetizer is important, as is its dessert. In this chapter, we'll extend our guidance on prompts to the race conversation's main course.

78

There are a few pitfalls we want to avoid:

- **Overguiding in your prompt:** Think about survey questions that are clearly pushing the respondent to choose one answer over another. We want to trust our students, the process of the conversation, and ourselves as facilitators enough to begin with a prompt that allows students the chance to explore their thinking and understanding. For example, asking "Do you think it was wrong when the character did _____?" will frequently set students up to think we want them to say yes. As a result, students will often agree, regardless of their thoughts. Keeping our prompts open-ended can help. Instead of the above option, we can say, "What did you think when the character did _____?" or "Why do you think the character did _____?" Those prompts open the door more widely for students' thoughts.

- **Not focusing students' attention on each other's *ideas*:** There is a big difference between "Do you agree with Sandra?" and "Do you agree with Sandra's idea that _____?" The former prompt's imprecise language has the potential to make an honest critique feel like a personal invalidation. The latter allows Sandra to retain her dignity even as her classmates are invited to thoughtfully critique her point. Instead of answering, "Sandra is wrong!" students might more productively say, "I don't see it the same way. I see _____."

- **Not encouraging the use of good data:** So often, in trying to center and validate students' opinions, we forget to push them toward important, relevant data. This is especially true when students find themselves with conflicting opinions— as we will show at length in Chapter 5's conversation about voting rights. Which side is "right"? What does "right" even mean in this context? Quality race conversations push students toward inquiry and, for our older elementary students, *research* into source material that supports, complicates, or debunks casual opinions.

79

- **Placing too much weight on individual conversations:**
  A specific race conversation will not be the one and only
  conversation. As we'll address next, layering and threading will
  help alleviate some of the need to make *every* race conversation life
  changing. We need to keep in mind where we have been and where
  we will go as we move into a specific conversation. We do well to
  plan our prompts so that they "build on" and "build forward."

- **Not providing enough time:** Different students need different
  amounts of time to tackle certain prompts. We should make
  sure that we have given students clear ways to communicate that
  they need more time to respond thoughtfully to what they've
  been asked, whether they've been asked to respond in writing or
  verbally. (One useful method is the "fist of five," where students
  are encouraged to hold up fingers for the number of minutes they
  need to finish processing.)

Let's explore an example of some thoughtful prompting. Jen's fourth
graders study Virginia history, and the history of voting rights plays a big role
in that. She once used prints from the *Picturing America* project from the
National Endowment for the Humanities as a source for the students to discuss. Jen displayed both George Caleb Bingham's *The County Election* from
1852 (Figure 3.1) and James Karales's photograph *Selma-to-Montgomery
March for Voting Rights* from 1965 (Figure 3.2). To open the conversation,
she pointed out to students that the painting was created before the Civil
War, more than one hundred years before the photograph was taken.
She then asked them, "What do you notice? What do you wonder?" This
prompt did not overguide. It has a low floor (it was easy to respond in some way) and a high ceiling (the thinking
can get quite complex.) In addition, such a prompt allowed Jen to gather
information on what background knowledge her students already had,
while also pushing them to critically analyze the images.

> A specific race conversation will not be the one and only conversation.

Students noticed and wondered about the differences between a painting and a photograph (re-creation versus a capture of reality). Another
quick observation was that in the painting, everyone is White, but in the

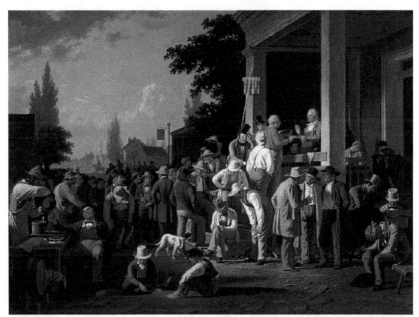

FIGURE 3.1
The County Election (1852) by George Caleb Bingham

FIGURE 3.2
Selma-to-Montgomery March for Voting Rights (1965)
by James Karales

photograph, most of the people are Black. Once students began noticing and recognized the differences between the two images, the conversation was off and going. The students asked questions about why the people in each image were mostly (if not all) of one race. They wondered about what was happening in the images and why the people were gathered. If they didn't get started on their own, Jen jumped in and asked students why they thought the groups were mostly White or mostly Black. Again, a simple "why" does not overguide.

"LAYERING" RACE INTO UNEXPECTED CONVERSATIONS

Matt loves to remind educators that a book doesn't need to be a "race" book to inspire good race conversations. Upper-elementary kids might enjoy reading *Stamped, The Hate U Give*, or *Dear Martin*, but they don't need to read these books in order to discuss systemic racism. Our littlest learners might enjoy reading *I Am Enough, Black Girl Magic*, or *We're Different, We're the Same*, but they don't need to read these books to spark an appreciation for diversity and self-love. Students should learn directly about multiple civil rights eras; but a particular social studies lesson doesn't *need* to be about the sixties-era Civil Rights Movement or antebellum enslavement for students to discuss the resilience of the oppressed. Our students should learn to appreciate art and music from many cultures, but the "text" in any one art class doesn't *need* to be from an artist of color for students to explore how it may have been influenced by such artists.

Oftentimes, there is an interesting microdiscussion that we can *layer* into lessons that don't traditionally engage race. When we do, race becomes less of a standalone subject and more of a thoughtful *lens* through which students view many relevant issues. In other words, race doesn't need to be any one lesson's main course. It can just be the seasoning that makes seemingly unrelated lessons just that much more interesting.

Layering with elementary students

In many ways, the greatest challenge in layering our curriculum is us. The great majority of elementary teachers are, like Jen, White women. It makes sense that we might not have the breadth and depth of knowledge necessary to meaningfully layer race into parts of our curriculum that do not traditionally engage it. We need to both recognize and remedy this.

The first step is educating ourselves. There are many ways to go about doing this, and trying a variety of them can be extra helpful.

1. **Read children's books by authors and illustrators of color.** These can be books that specifically address race and help us better understand its role in our history and current society. Or they can be books about characters of color that are not explicitly about racial issues. Not only will these books build our knowledge, but they will also help us offer students more diverse, and therefore representative, options for their reading.

2. **Read adult books by authors of color.** Read books that give you context for how race has impacted our society from the beginning. Read books that show you what it means to be a person of color in our country today. Read books that highlight people of color and their contributions.

3. **Follow people of color on social media.** Follow hashtags that educate about race in our country. Join online groups and sign up for newsletters that do the same. When you find a good source online, look for connected resources. Build your network so that your online time is broadening and deepening your knowledge.

4. **Consider the media you consume.** Are the TV shows and movies you watch full of White characters? Written and directed by White people? What about the music or podcasts you listen to? Try expanding your horizons by searching out options created by people of color. You'll quickly find that even "popular" or "mainstream" media created by people of color will be an education for you.

As our knowledge base grows, we will be in a stronger position to layer our curriculum for (and with) our students.

A Couple Of Examples from Jen's Classroom:

1. During a science unit on the solar system, you can introduce your students to Gladys West, a Black woman who created an accurate model of the earth through mathematics and programming. That model was foundational in the creation of GPS.

2. As students learn about the early 1900s and the various magnates who greatly impacted that time, you can teach them about Belle da Costa Greene, J. P. Morgan's personal librarian. She was able to thrive in that position, and in high society, because she passed as White rather than living as a Black woman.

Planning a future unit of study should include seeing if we can layer race into our class discussions. If we can't, that's okay! But if we *can*, where? Are there individuals we can highlight? Are there art, music, dance, or theater styles we can share that are related? Are there missing voices and perspectives that we can shine a spotlight on? We don't have to do the deepest dive every time; just chatting about a race connection for three minutes adds a special layer of complexity for our students—with the added benefit of offering an unexpected hook for students of color to latch their interest to.

THREADING RACE CONVERSATIONS TOGETHER

In addition to layering race into conversations in unexpected ways, we sometimes have the opportunity to connect—or "thread"—race conversations throughout the course of the school year—building especially upon discussions that caught kids' attention. As with many other perspectives, rich understandings about race can be sequentially developed. Students can analyze an issue through a race lens, discuss something cool about their observations, then, weeks later, see the same issue from a different angle and discuss how their thinking has been impacted. Texts can be selected with these connections in mind. In this manner, students are constantly applying what they've previously discussed to fresh contexts and new conversations.

Threading with elementary students

One of the joys of working with elementary students is the ability to connect lessons across time and across content areas. Teaching the same students all day and all year gives us many opportunities to help students see how their learning ties together. Let's explore one possibility.

Imagine starting with Constitution Day, something we're all required to teach (US Department of Education 2005), and, over time, continuing a discussion of how the makeup of our founders (wealthy White men) impacted the United States' begin-

> Teaching the same students all day and all year gives us many opportunities to help students see how their learning ties together.

nings, has impacted our history, and impacts us today. We might kick off the discussion by showing students an image of the people who signed the Constitution. We could ask them, "What do you notice? What do you wonder?" They'll notice that everyone in the room is male and White. We can share that they were also landowners, which meant they were wealthy. Students will often then have many other questions or thoughts to share. (This is a conversation from Jen's classroom, a moment we'll explore in greater detail in Chapter 5 of this book.)

Many elementary social studies curriculums start the year off with a focus on citizenship, rules and laws, and communities. Throughout this unit of study, our students might continue to explore how our society is impacted by having been created, structurally at least, by wealthy White men. A district's social studies unit may or may not address this, but our students will be able to keep that important point in mind as they explore what it means to be a community, what defines a good citizen, or what laws and rules they follow regularly.

As the year goes on, a curriculum might highlight certain historical figures, scientists, mathematicians, and writers. If, as is quite common, the majority of those individuals are/were White men, our students might connect this observation to their continuing conversation about the formation of our country. They can notice that it is possible that White men had opportunities to succeed, and therefore to be noted in our history in ways that women and people of color did not.

School holidays are another time we can continue to thread this conversation. Some districts have made a deliberate effort to schedule school holidays around a wide range of religions. Other districts have not. Students might notice that classmates miss days for Diwali or Eid and consider why those days are school days and Christmas is not.

Books, both those students are required to read (if that is the case in your school) and ones they choose, also offer an avenue for continuing the conversation. What percentage of the authors they read or have available to them are White men? What percentage of the main characters in their books are White males? What percentage of those main characters are wealthy or well-off? If we are threading this conversation successfully from early in the year, students will begin to ask these questions and make these connections independently. That's what we're really hoping will happen, that students gain the skills to look at their learning and their world with a critical lens. That they are able to question what they are taught, what they are told, and what they see happening around them. Threading, building that conversation across time, is a powerful way to help students develop these skills.

REFLECTING AND ASSESSING OVER TIME

Ultimately, we are planting seeds. When we are lucky, those seeds sprout quickly, and we are able to see the fruits of our labor. Often, those seeds are slower growing. The results take time, and we must have faith in the work we are doing. In her first year of teaching, many years ago, this was definitely not a lesson Jen understood. She taught fourth graders then, and as part of the study of Virginia's history, she read them Patricia Polacco's picture book *Pink and Say*. Polacco tells a family story of Sheldon ("Say"), a wounded young White Union soldier who is rescued by Pinkus ("Pink"), a young Black Union soldier. They go to Pink's mother for Say to heal, but marauding Confederate troops arrive. Pink's mother is killed, and the boys are captured. In Jen's naivete, she was concerned that her young students would not fully grasp the depth of the danger faced by the characters in this story or the weight of what the young Black soldier and his enslaved mother were doing in the South during the Civil War.

She viewed this book as *the* race lesson she was teaching them, rather than seeing it in a larger context, layering and threading through their year. As a result, she hammered at the story's sad angles and left her students, many of them survivors of their own intense traumas, in tears. (Thank goodness for kind, patient, strong school counselors who knew far better than she how to support her students in that moment.) Her goal—a worthy one, we think—was for her students to understand the heavy role race played in our ancestors' lives and, by extension, the role it still plays in our lives. That lesson was definitely not learned that day, unfortunately. It was also, to be completely honest, unlikely to be learned in any one day.

Jen had to learn to trust that, over time and with a layered and threaded curriculum, these big ideas would be engaged and understood—but at a pace that made the most sense for kids' well-being. But how can we know that our students are gaining this deep understanding? Especially when we're dealing with really young children, it can be hard to assess their understanding because they aren't yet fully able to express their thinking in writing. How we determine what students are understanding from a conversation depends a great deal on the ages of the students.

For upper elementary

Many of the ideas that Matt shared in *Not Light* can be quite effective with upper-elementary students. As adults and mature thinkers, we need to model our own reflection processes. During conversations, we can respond to and build upon our students' ideas. This requires clearly showing students when (and how) *their* thinking is impacting and, quite possibly, changing *our* thinking. There are many ways to describe our thought process for older elementary students. Here are some examples:

- I heard Ashley say _____, and that makes me wonder about _____.

- That's something I hadn't thought about, Rameen. I am going to think about that some more.

- Ashley just shared how Rameen's idea made her think about this in a new way. That's really exciting!

87

One of the most powerful options we can offer our students is to have them pause during or after conversations and write their reflections. Pausing to write during conversations can be important, but it is often challenging for young learners to pivot back and forth between partici-pating in the conversation and writing about their thinking. If we do choose to have our students reflect during a conversation, we can have everyone stop for a few minutes to write and then return to the discussion. This is especially useful if the talk is getting heated or if some really crucial points have been made. Giving students some time to think through what they're hearing and write down their thoughts can push the conversation to the next level when they resume.

Writing after a conversation accomplishes two things. It offers students a chance to gain some closure on what could be a weighty topic. Making them stop, slow down their thoughts, and write their reflections can force students to organize their ideas and look at them through new lenses, ones that might not have been available in the midst of ideas flying around. Students can end the lesson with a deeper understanding by sitting with their own thoughts for a bit before moving on to whatever is next in the day. Taking this time to write can also offer us a window into our students' understanding. Because this writing happens after a conversation, in a slower, more individual moment, we may get a different perspective on what our students are thinking than we see during the conversation.

For middle elementary

To reflect on conversations and write meaningfully about their think-ing, students in this age range may need slightly more guidance than older students. Here are some example prompts that provide such support:

- When _____ said _____, it made me think . . .
- I want to add on to what _____ said . . .
- I agree (or disagree) with _____ because . . .

We may not want to ask these students to write as often as we might ask older students, but it is still an option that can serve us and our learners well. It is often helpful for us to write down—for ourselves—what we would hope to see our students understand. We can imagine a stellar example, a typical grade-level example, and an example that would show a student needed more support. When we have been able to state to ourselves where we want our students to be after the conversation, we can better determine what questions or sentence-starters to offer them for their written reflections.

For our youngest learners

Assessing what our youngest students "get" from an extended threaded conversation is more challenging than gauging our older students' comprehension. There are, however, a couple of useful possibilities. One option is to meet with a small group of our students or to meet with them one-on-one and get their reflections verbally. We can consider our question or prompt in the same way that teachers of middle-elementary students might do—we just have to talk with the students rather than have them write. One-on-one is the ideal situation to gain insight, but depending on class size and the daily schedule, that may not be an option. A small group will also work well, as more students will have the opportunity (and hopefully the willingness) to speak than they would in a whole-class conversation.

If even that seems difficult in a setting, and students have technology available (as most do, these days), they can voice-record their reflections. We can record the prompt or question in our online learning management system or other location that is familiar to our students, and they can record themselves talking about their thinking. This option will require more time outside of class, but it does offer us insight into every student and their development and understanding of the ideas they've been discussing.

Whether we record class conversations, take notes during them, have students write after them, or talk with our students to get their thinking, we need to find a way that works for us to assess students' progress throughout threaded conversations. Whatever tool or system we use, these formative assessments allow us to have some understanding of our students' knowledge and growth. That is crucial for knowing how to continue to support and nudge them forward.

TALKING ABOUT OPPRESSION

Planning meaningful classroom race conversations can be emotionally exhausting, especially when it requires us to take deeper dives into racism's long history and then make decisions about what to put in front of kids. Some of us are rightfully worried that, as we engage some understandably heavy subject matter, we might pass our personal exhaustion onto our students. As we fret about this, however, we might miss both a key reflection and some wonderful opportunities.

The reflection

Race conversations might not, by definition, *need* to center oppression. Now, readers, don't you dare go around saying, "Jen and Matt said, 'Stop talking about racism.'" Race is a social construct that was created—rather recently in human history—to uphold White supremacy. This is not our opinion or a political stance; this is a historically verifiable fact. Because of this root connection, when we have students discuss *race*, they are likely, eventually, to end up discussing *racism*. What we have noticed, however, is that nearly *all* classroom race conversations start by centering some form of oppression. This means that, most of the time, Black and brown students learn about Black and brown experiences only as they relate to struggles and successes against White oppression. It's worth our time to reflect upon the impact of this association for students of all racial and cultural backgrounds.

THE OPPORTUNITIES

Instead of always centering oppression, let's try taking a different approach to race conversations. Here are some ideas:

1. Blend plenty of cultural discussions that do not immediately center White supremacy into our curriculum. For instance, we can discuss what makes jazz and hip-hop cool, what makes various cuisines unique, and what makes different holidays special.

2. Plan discussions about Black and brown joy that is not linked to overcoming oppression but is just a natural expression of Black and brown humanity. For instance, when exploring the beauty

of different hair styling conventions, we can prompt from books like *Hair Love*, by Matthew A. Cherry and Vashti Harrison, or *Cool Cuts*, by Mechal Renee Roe.

3. Examine the achievements of people of color on their own merits. Black and brown folks don't exist merely to be compared to famous White folks in similar fields. For instance, we can teach about Little Richard without centering the idea that he inspired Elvis Presley. He has an intriguing story of his own that deserves to take up space. So does Jackie Robinson, whose story is just as interesting without centering his influential manager Branch Rickey or his kind teammate Pee Wee Reese. Yes, their relationships with White folks were important, but these Black men brought more than enough to the table on their own!

"But that's not fair!"

Even though we should make this special effort to not *only* center oppression, let's face it: most race conversations will eventually get there. Facing and recognizing injustice or, as elementary students are likely to say, things that "are not fair," can be hard for us, even as adults. We can feel an uncomfortable sense of smallness, and even sometimes powerlessness in the face of enemies as complex as White supremacy. As adults, we may have an understanding of *why* we feel that way, and we might have learned strategies for coping with those difficult feelings. Children often feel this same frustration with big things that are not fair, *but often without the same coping strategies*. Similarly, because many of the more obvious "things we can do about it" are things *only adults* can do (like vote), younger students can feel even more powerless in the face of racism.

Because of this, we end this chapter in much the same way we began, by reminding teachers to design race conversations around what *kids* need.

We can support students in their desire to take action. When young children find that things are not fair, they frequently want to remedy the situation. Vivian Vasquez writes about this in *Negotiating Critical Literacies with Young Children*: "My role was not to tell the children what to think or how to act, but based on their inquiries, to offer alternate ways of taking action and a way of naming their world within the stance they chose to take" (2014, 121–122). Vasquez is describing this work with very young children, mostly four-year-olds. She offers them surveys, petitions, and letter writing as ways to address the inequities and "not fairness" that they see. As Vasquez notes, our role is not to tell students what to do but to support them in their plan of action. Frequently, the actions taken by elementary students, as by Vasquez's young learners, will not result in significant change. That is not actually the goal. Instead, we hope our students see their learning as active, as something that has meaning beyond the classroom. Taking action, regardless of the result, gives their work meaning.

We can help students use their understanding of racism and its impact to become more critical thinkers and observers of their world. As students tackle difficult questions and discuss challenging issues, they will begin to see the same questions and issues in their smaller world. After reading books about students who do not feel like they fit in, students might make connections to their school or district's dress code and the ways in which it singles out groups by race or gender. This work will give students the skills to look at the world around them with a critical lens.

A STUDY OF CONVERSATIONS

Throughout the first three chapters, we have attempted to weave in plenty of real-life classroom examples. Knowing that it is always important to see theories in practice, the three chapters in Part 2 will each offer a detailed description of a race conversation from Jen's classroom. In Part 2 of *Not Light*, Matt described race conversations in his high school classes in a "bell to bell" manner, trying to capture every detail of a single class period's discussion. This approach, however, doesn't quite mirror an elementary teacher's experience, so the examples from Jen's classroom will describe conversation threads that stretch over a series of days or weeks. These chapters will show, in a very true sense, what it means to help kids "keep on talking" about race throughout a school year.

Each of these conversations has been attempted in Jen's classroom at least five times, in the past fifteen years, with students in kindergarten and in first, third, fourth, and fifth grades. They are composite conversations: while the interactions between students are real, they may have taken place over a series of years. (For instance, exchanges between classmates that may have occurred in different years might appear here to have happened in the same class period.) Some of these race conversations have succeeded, and others have failed. The highs have been spectacular, the lows humbling. We describe not only the wins but also the losses, the bad decisions, the unlucky variables. As you read these examples, please take into account your own interpersonal strengths and your students' cultural and academic backgrounds. The conversations you'll have with your students will likely look and sound different from Jen's, but it is our hope that the conversations you'll read about in Part 2 will help you to visualize what these conversations might look like in your classroom.

CHAPTER 4

NAMES AND IDENTITIES IN PRESCHOOL AND EARLY ELEMENTARY

C hapter 1 of this book showed how crucial it is for us to help students develop and practice listening skills. It also showed how to help students create networks of relationships that allow them to feel safe enough to earnestly participate in race conversations. These goals are especially important in early elementary (PreK–1), which sets the foundation for the rest of students' experience in school.

I invest a lot of energy in the first weeks of the school year, developing an atmosphere in which these youngest elementary students can learn *how* to engage in these conversations. The race conversations that happen with early-elementary students are carefully chosen, their many possible variations carefully considered. Each is rooted in strong personal connections for my students and is carefully designed to help them develop connections with each other.

OUR NAME STORIES

Early in the school year, I gathered my young learners on the carpet, showing them the cover of *Alma and How She Got Her Name* by Juana Martinez-Neal. This is a fictional picture book about a girl with the name

Alma Sofia Esperanza José Pura Candela. As the students take a look at the cover, I read the title and ask, "What do you expect from this book? What are you thinking about it?"

I then began reading. At the beginning of the book, Alma tells her father that her name is too long. I paused the story to ask students what they think of Alma's name. *Does it seem too long? What do they think of her name?*

Some students shared that Alma's name was *absolutely* too long, she had *so* many names! Other students, mostly Latinx students, felt that Alma's name was just right, or maybe a *tad* bit on the long side. They all wanted to hear more about her name, so I continued reading. As the book continues, Alma's father tells her where each of her names comes from, starting with "Sofia." Each of Alma's names comes from an ancestor, and she connects with special things about each of them and embraces each of her names.

> The race conversations that happen with early-elementary students are carefully chosen, their many possible variations carefully considered.

As I read, students' faces lit up, and some couldn't help calling out their connections:

- "I'm named after my grandmother too!"

- "I like to draw. Just like Alma!"

- "I'm learning to read! I'm like Sofia!"

As I heard these comments, I nodded to acknowledge my student's connections—but I didn't stop reading. I had a plan for where I would stop mid-book, and I didn't want to stop too early. I knew these young learners would have a lot to say, and if I opted to stop too often, we would not get through the book. I continued until I finished reading about all of Alma's names except her first one. Stopping to talk at strategic points throughout the book gives young learners a chance to more deeply process the story and ideas as they emerge. They don't have to hold on to the entire story before they get the chance to talk through their ideas about it. When we reached this first planned stopping point, I said to them,

"Turn and talk with a partner about your thinking about Alma's name now that we've learned more about it."

CONNECTING WITH TEXTS: FROM PARTNER TALK TO WHOLE-CLASS CONVERSATIONS

It was clear, through the connections they'd called out while I read, that my students needed some time to speak through their thinking about *Alma and How She Got Her Name*. Their minds had filled up with reactions to the book, and turning to a partner would give everyone an opportunity to release a bit of this pressure. Without that opportunity, some students would likely have difficulty listening both patiently and actively to their classmates when we attempted to discuss the book as a whole class.

With their partners, students repeated many of the comments they had called out during the reading and shared other thoughts they had managed to keep to themselves.

When students turned back to discuss with the whole group, they shared lots of connections to Alma. Franklin started off the sharing by saying, "I'm named after my daddy too. His name is Franklin."

Lina kept things going: "I'm not named after anybody, but I love books, just like Alma."

There were many students who wanted the chance to share their thoughts, so we kept listening to each other. Eventually, however, I was able to finish the book. At the end, Alma's dad tells her that he picked her first name because it was unique to her, and she would get to make her own story. The author includes a short note at the very end about her own name and her shifting feelings about it. Then she writes, "What is the story of your name? What story would you like it to tell?"

I told students that we would be talking more about their names in the coming days. "Your next task is to talk with your family about your name," I explained. "You can ask why you were given the name you were given. You can find out more about any connections your name has to your family and ancestors or to your culture." Students squirmed on the carpet with excitement about learning more about their names, the prospect of sharing with their classmates, and learning about classmates' names as well.

By that point, we had been gathered on the carpet for about twenty-five minutes. This was as long as I thought these students would be able to sit comfortably and focus, especially this early in the school year, so we moved on to other parts of our day, knowing we'd be back to this conversation soon.

That afternoon, I emailed families to share details about our conversation that morning and to let them know that their child might be asking about names (or that they could initiate a chat about names with their child, in case that young person had forgotten about it). This kind of invitation to families to continue or supplement a cultural conversation was described in Chapter 1's section on house talk. In this email, I emphasized that families and children could share whatever they wanted about their names and histories. I was sure to note that they did not *have* to share anything at all if that was their preference. Name stories can carry a lot of weight. I wanted families to be able to share or not, whatever they thought would be best for their child.

CONNECTING TO THE STANDARDS

As teachers well know, understanding our standards and how we will connect them to our race conversations is critical. While your standards may differ from the Virginia Standards of Learning that Jen teaches, these "Connecting to the Standards" boxes throughout Part 2 of this book are designed to help you think about the ways you can connect standards to the work of talking about race.

KINDERGARTEN ENGLISH STANDARDS

K.1 The student will build oral communication skills.

  f) Discuss various texts and topics collaboratively and with partners.

  i) Ask how and why questions to seek help, get information or clarify information.

K.7 The student will expand vocabulary and use of word meanings.

   a) Discuss meanings of words.

   b) Increase vocabulary by listening to a variety of texts read aloud.

(Virginia Department of Education 2017, 7)

SHARING OUR STORIES

In the following days, many students went back to the book on their own during our independent reading time. They retold the story as they reviewed the pictures, often sitting with a friend or two and talking about Alma and her various names. The book had clearly made an impact.

Nearly a week later, after I'd given families a chance to discuss their children's names, it seemed like a good time to return to our discussion thread. Picking up *Alma and How She Got Her Name* again, I reminded students of how Alma had been given each of her names. I then told them, "I am the exact opposite of Alma. I only have three names. My last name is the same as my parents'. My first and middle names were names my parents thought were pretty. They did not have any connection to family or to anything else." After my students reacted to this, I added, "I like my names, all three of them, but I often feel a little disappointed that there's no story behind them. So both of my children, Kate and Charlie, have first and middle names that have stories behind them. Maybe I'll share those stories with you all sometime soon, but right now, I want us to focus on *your* stories. How many of you have had a chance to talk with your family about your name?" I asked. This wording was intentional; solidly connecting my lived experience to our conversation, while decentering this experience in favor of my students'. We described this goal in Chapter 3.

Most students eagerly raised their hands, while a few looked slightly chagrined or uncomfortable. As I saw their faces register discomfort, I realized that, while I had intentionally decentered myself, I still should have phrased the warm-up prompt differently. I should have instead asked, "Who *wants* to share what they've learned about their name from their family?" This way I could have gotten things started without sounding as if I were shaming students who had not broached the name conversation at home. By phrasing it as "How many of you," I had inadvertently singled out those who had not yet done so.

I attempted to recover. "We're going to start this conversation today, but if you haven't gotten to talk about your name yet, there's still time. We won't be finished with the conversation today. We'll be talking more about this, and you can share whenever you're ready. And if you prefer not to share, that's okay too." I thought, especially based on some students' embarrassed reactions, that some families had not yet had this conversation, and I did not want students to feel badly about that. I wanted them to know that the window was still open for them. Some families might never have the conversation, for a variety of reasons. They may rarely have had time to be together as a family, depending on work and school schedules and other family commitments, and this conversation might not have risen to the top of their list in the family times they did have. Some families may not have wanted to discuss the history of their child's name. Some students may have lived with a caregiver who did not name them and did not know the story of their name. As previously noted, name stories are intimate. Families may not have been ready to share the stories behind the name. Telling students that we would discuss more later and that they did not have to share at all took some of the burden off of them.

Pushing forward despite my mistake, I asked, "Is anyone ready to share the story of their name?"

Wyatt waved his hand in the air. "My name comes from my granddad," he said. "His name is Wyatt, just like me!"

I turned to our chart paper and started writing. At the top, I wrote, "Our Name Stories," and below that, "Family Names." I wrote "Wyatt" to start that list. "Wyatt's name comes from someone else in his family," I told my students. "He is named after his granddad. Maybe some others of you are named after someone in your family."

Sophie shared that she got her name because it was her mother's middle name. I added Sophie's name to our chart under Wyatt's. Diego told us that he was named after his dad, and his name went up under Sophie's. A few other students shared their names' connections to their families, and I added each as we went along. Then I asked, "Does anyone have a different story about their name? Did anyone get their name for a *different* reason?"

Christopher raised his hand and said, "I'm named Christopher because my birthday is the same day as Saint Christopher's Day."

I paused for a moment, considering what heading to put on our chart for this one. I decided to ask Christopher for some more information before choosing. "Christopher, can you tell us more about that?"

"Umm," he said. "Well, ummm, my birthday is July 25, and that is Saint Christopher's Day, so my mom named me Christopher."

"Do you know anything about Saint Christopher?" I asked him.

"Not really," he answered, "but my mom has a necklace with him on it."

"It sounds like he's pretty important to your family." I said. "I want to be sure I understand your name. You are named after Saint Christopher because of your birthday. Saint Christopher is a part of your religion?"

"Yeah, we talked about him at church," Christopher answered.

I decided to write "Religious Names" on our chart and put Christopher's name under it. "Does anyone else have a name that comes from their religion?" I asked.

Hannah said, "My name comes from the Bible. My mom also really likes that my name is a special word because it's the same from the front or the back." I chuckled as I wrote Hannah's name on the chart. I also wanted to be sure that her classmates understood what she meant. I pointed at her name and asked her to explain more to us about that. She walked up to the chart and pointed at the letters in her name. "My name is H-A-N-N-A-H, but if I start at the end, it is still H-A-N-N-A-H."

Her classmates were fascinated. Some stared at her name in awe. Others made comments, like "Oh! Whoa!"

I paused long enough to explain, "That means Hannah's name is a palindrome. Palindromes are special words that are spelled the same forward and backward. That is a pretty amazing thing to have in your name." Hannah sat up a little taller and grinned.

David added that his name also came from the Bible, and I wrote it on the chart.

I asked if anyone else wanted to share where their name came from. Muska told us that her name means "smile." She said, "My mom was so excited when I was born. She kept smiling. So she named me Muska." I wrote "Meaning Names" on the chart and put Muska's there.

"That's like me!" Jayden said. "My name means thankful. That's why my mom and dad named me Jayden." I added his name to the chart.

Jose explained that his name came from where his mom was born. "She's from a town in Guatemala that is called Jose," he said. I wrote "Place Names" on our chart and added Jose's name. We had now collected names in four categories: Family Names, Religious Names, Meaning Names, and Place Names.

Cindy raised her hand. "My name doesn't go in any of those groups. I don't know about my name because I have two names." She paused and we waited, looking at her as she thought about what she wanted to say. "Cindy is my American name. I have a Vietnamese name too."

I added one more section to our chart, "Cultural/Language Names," and wrote "Cindy" under it. Then I turned back to Cindy and said, "You gave us another group for our chart. Do you want to talk about your two names?"

She paused, thinking about my question, and said, "Well, I was born in Vietnam, and my parents named me Tuyen. When I was little, we came here, and they thought my name might not be okay here. So they picked "Cindy." So I have two names."

I thanked Cindy for helping us understand that. Some students, in Cindy's shoes, might have been unsettled about what they'd just shared. Cindy did not seem to be bothered by it, an assessment I made based on my familiarity with her body language. Of course, I could easily have been

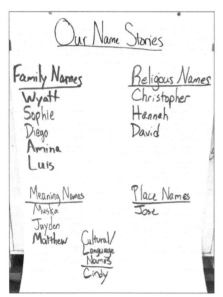

FIGURE 4.1
"Our Name Stories" chart from Jen's kindergarten classroom

wrong, so I did make a mental note to keep an eye on Cindy as our name conversations continued. We all regularly try to read how our students are handling situations based on the best information we have at the time (a student's body language, etc.). We have to. They aren't going to knowingly communicate their emotions in every moment. Our read of their emotional reactions isn't always going to be correct. But our interpretive muscles *can* be strengthened by the deliberate community building (a focus on listening and house talk activities) described in Chapter 1. We just have to be ready to adapt either when we misread a student or when they react in a way we don't anticipate.

> My goal was to spark my students' curiosity and get them anticipating how we might build upon this increasingly complex conversation.

We reviewed our list. We looked at each of the different categories and thought about the names we saw. I again encouraged my students to continue the conversation at home, this time asking about the names of other people in their household. I ended with "This was such an interesting conversation. Tomorrow we'll keep talking about this, especially thinking about what Cindy shared with us about her experience with her name." My goal was to spark my students' curiosity and get them anticipating how we might build upon this increasingly complex conversation.

NAMES AND CULTURE

When we returned to our discussion thread the following day, I pointed back at our chart. I started off by asking, "Does anyone want to share about other names in their house? Do you want to share about anyone else whose name might fit somewhere here?"

Not surprisingly, many did! Students shared about parents or siblings who had family names or names that carried a certain meaning. They responded to each other as they heard their classmates share names that were the same as names in their own families. "My mom has the same name as your sister!" and similar comments were called out.

I allowed a few minutes of this casual discussion to recenter us in our thinking about names, their importance, and where they came from. Then I shared another book with my class. *Your Name Is a Song*, written by Jamilah

Thompkins-Bigelow and illustrated by Luisa Uribe, is a beautiful book, both visually and aurally. In it, a young girl, whose name is not shared until the very end of the book, is angry because no one at school can say her name properly. On their walk home from school, her mother suggests that she tell her teacher that her "name is a song," something the girl chafes at. Her mother sings some names for her. As they continue walking home, the girl mentions multiple moments in her day when others had trouble with her name. With each story, her mom adds to her understanding of the power of names. She tells the girl that names come from the heart, that names can have fire and strength, and that names come from dreamers. With each new idea, her mother gives new names as examples. These names are all listed at the end of the book, along with their origin and meaning. Thompkins-Bigelow includes names from all around the world.

The book gently but powerfully addresses the challenges of having a name that doesn't fit the restrictive norms of a Eurocentric society. I hoped that Cindy would connect with this book, and by the looks of it, she did. I asked students what they were thinking, and then specifically asked whether they had ever felt like this girl or maybe like some of her classmates who had shared similar name stories.

Cindy responded, "A lot of people have trouble saying my last name. They don't say it right." I asked her to say her last name for us. She said, "It's Nguyen [pronounced 'win']." I thanked her for sharing this and for making sure we knew how to say her name correctly.

David raised his hand. "My parents say my name differently than everyone else." I asked him if he could tell us a little more about that. So he continued, "My mom calls me 'David' [pronounced 'Dah-veed'], but at school everyone says 'David' [pronounced 'Day-vid')."

"Thank you for sharing that, David." I said, as I noticed Gladis waving her hand in the air. I nodded at her, and she jumped right in.

"Me too!" she said. "My name is Gladis [pronounced 'Glah-dees'], but everyone says it like 'Gladys' ['Gla-dis']! That's not my name!"

"Thank you, Gladis, for sharing that with us. It sounds like you can connect with the girl in our book. People have trouble with her name, and people have trouble with your name, too," I said. Gladis vigorously nodded her head in agreement.

I continued, "David, Gladis, and Cindy, we can see how the girl in our book feels when people have trouble with her name. Would you be willing to share how you feel when this happens to you?" (I carefully asked "would you be willing," to be sure they didn't feel they had to speak about something that might be difficult or uncomfortable for them.)

Gladis was ready to share her thoughts. "It's bad!" she said. "It makes me feel bad when people say my name wrong. I don't like it." David nodded in agreement.

Cindy continued, "It's okay. I just have one name at home and one name at school."

The rest of the class had been watching these three students closely. It was clear they were thinking about their friends' names.

I had previously noticed the challenges with Gladis's and David's names. When they said their names to others, they pronounced them as they heard them at home, as their names were meant to be said. Many of the adults in our school building, however, pronounced them in a more Americanized way. As a result, many of their classmates, although not all, did the same. I was careful to pronounce their names as they did, but I had not specifically addressed the issue. Now, hearing them share, I decided to not only address it in this conversation but to follow up with other adults in the building when they Americanized these names. I wish I'd had a conversation with Gladis and David sooner. I had been hesitant to correct other adults because I did not know what Gladis and David would have wanted me to do. If I had asked them about it as soon as I was noticing the issue, I would have corrected others sooner, and I regretted not doing so.

In this moment, I wanted to be sure we all had these names straight, as well as those of the rest of the students. "Let's practice saying these names the way our friends say them," I said. I looked at Gladis and asked her to say her name. She did so, and we all repeated it together. She smiled and nodded. We did the same with David.

I looked at Cindy and asked, "You have two names. Which one would you like us to use when we talk to you?" She thought for a moment, and we all waited. "Cindy," she responded. "That's my name at school." As a Jennifer, I must have gone through every possible iteration of that name in my K–12 years (Jen, Jenn, Jenny, Jenni, and who knows what else). I appreciate all of the teachers who were respectful and generous and used whatever version of my name I requested. Again, names are intimate. Allowing our students to determine what they want to be called is important. I can't speak to Cindy's reasons for choosing that name for school, but we, as her class, could respect it.

> Allowing our students to determine what they want to be called is important. I can't speak to Cindy's reasons for choosing that name for school, but we, as her class, could respect it.

After thanking Cindy, I looked at the rest of the class. "Is there anyone else who would like us to practice saying their name to be sure we're pronouncing it properly?" I felt pretty confident that no one else was having their name mispronounced on a regular basis, but I did not want to move forward on that assumption, in case it was wrong.

Not surprisingly, almost every student wanted us to practice saying their name properly! So we took a few minutes while each student carefully said their name to us and we repeated it.

ONGOING CONVERSATIONS

It's rare that meaningful conversations in early-elementary classrooms come to a definite end. Students come back to ideas from these conversations again and again, as they make connections or have new questions. After this conversation, I noticed my students being more aware of each other's names. Some of them noticed that certain classmates had two last names while others only had one. I overheard students wondering aloud why that might be. Based on our classroom conversation about names, they wondered if parents picked last names. Many of the students with two last names were Latinx. In many Latinx cultures, children are given the first last name from their mother and the second last name from their father, meaning each person has two last names, none of which, for father, mother, and child, are exactly the same. With so many different naming conventions and traditions, it was easy to see how young students might think that the last names had been picked, just as their first names had been.

Trying to help them understand, I asked students where their last names came from. I shouldn't have been surprised when they were unable to answer. The question had come out of their confusion. I had only added to the confusion by asking a question I could be fairly confident they weren't ready to answer. I paused for a moment and reconsidered my question. Then I asked, "Who has the same last name as you?"

Hannah shared that she had the exact same last name as both of her parents. Cindy said the same. Wyatt said he had the same name as his dad but not as his mom. Sophie explained that she had the same last name as her mom, but she didn't know what her dad's last name was because she didn't know him. David and Gladis each had different last names from both of their parents. I explained briefly that different cultures approach last names differently. I opted to do a quick sort of the students. Sorting them did two things. One, it allowed them to visually see whose last names were the same as their parents' and whose weren't. It also allowed these young children a chance to get up and move a bit, something that can be helpful in keeping their focus. Sitting on the carpet for more than ten or fifteen minutes can get challenging, so getting up to walk to a group can help.

I asked all those students who had the same last name as one or both of their parents to stand on one side of our carpet. I considered splitting out the students who shared with only one parent, but I did not want to stigmatize students who only had one parent. It's possible the students wouldn't have noticed or thought about it, but I did not want any student to be made to feel uncomfortable if it was avoidable. I asked those students who had a different last name from their parents to stand on the other side of the carpet. The kids hopped up and moved to one side or the other. Then I asked, "What do you notice?"

They all looked around at who was standing beside them and who was standing at the other end of our carpet. I waited silently, giving them time to process and think through what they were seeing. Gladis said, "All of us on this side speak Spanish."

"Yeah, we do," said Jayden. "So does Franklin, and he's on the other side."

I jumped in. "That's really interesting, Gladis and Jayden. You've noticed that over here, where everyone has a different last name from their

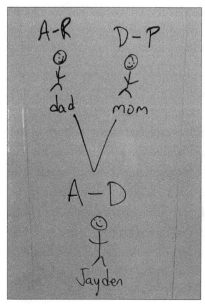

FIGURE 4.2
A whiteboard sketch helping students see where a classmate's last names come from

mom and dad, everyone speaks Spanish. Over there, where people have the same last name as their mom or dad, people speak different languages. Franklin speaks Spanish. Cindy speaks Vietnamese. It's not all the same."

I went on to explain that in many Latinx cultures, the mom and dad each give their children one of their last names. I worried this idea was a little abstract and might be confusing, so I had the students sit back down on the carpet and I grabbed a dry erase marker. On the board, I drew a quick stick figure and labeled it with "A-D." Those are the initials for Jayden's last names. Then I drew lines diagonally going up and away from the Jayden stick figure. I drew a stick figure at the top of each of those lines to represent his mom and dad. For his mom, I wrote "D-P" for her last initials. For his dad, I wrote "A-R." I said the names for the initials for each of those three people as I wrote. Then I drew diagonal lines up and away from his parents and added four more stick figures. I asked my students if they knew what the first initial would be for each of these people. With some wait time and pointing at the initials for Jayden and his parents, they were able to say that the dad on one side would start with *A* and the other dad's initials would start with *D*, and the two moms would start with *P* and *R*, respectively.

I told them, "I have an aunt who is from Spain. My cousins, like Jayden, have both my aunt and uncle's last names. I have the same last name as my parents. But I didn't change my last name when I got married. My husband and I have different last names. Our kids have their dad's last name. There are lots of different ways last names work for people. Sometimes that has to do with where they live or are from and how last names typically work there. Sometimes it has more to do with what their parents wanted to do. That was such an interesting thing for you all to notice! It'll be interesting to see what else you notice about names in the future."

As the year went on, I definitely heard conversations between students about names. They talked about the name of a substitute teacher in music and argued, gently and respectfully, about how to pronounce it. They noticed when new students or visitors to our classroom had one last name or two last names.

> Perhaps most interestingly, for the rest of the school year I noticed that, while David and Gladis still accepted their names being mispronounced, their classmates *did not*.

Perhaps most interestingly, for the rest of the school year I noticed that, while David and Gladis still accepted their names being mispronounced, their classmates *did not*. Once they had discussed names, thought about their importance, and worked to be sure they were saying everyone's correctly, they were quick to let adults know when they weren't doing so. They would—mostly politely—point out to teachers or other adults that they were not pronouncing David's or Gladis's name as it should be pronounced. While this was often a surprise to my colleagues, I am happy that their response was mostly to thank the student who spoke up, apologize to David or Gladis, and try to better remember the correct pronunciation.

REFLECTIONS ON OUR NAME CONVERSATIONS

None of my planned prompts in these name conversations explicitly addressed race, although, if students themselves had made explicit connections to race (as they made connections to ethnicity in the impromptu discussion of *last* names), I would have certainly encouraged them to explore those connections. However, my highest priority was to be sure I was following my students' lead, because name conversations are so personal and intimate. It is certainly possible that *some* of my students were thinking about how race impacted the choice of their name or the name of someone else but weren't ready to talk about it yet. It's important to remember that there's always tomorrow.

Furthermore, I was confident that, even though this name conversation didn't directly center race, thinking about our name stories would serve as a foundation for future race conversations. And sure enough, a little later in the year, a conversation about skin color built upon the habits established here.

SKIN COLOR AND SOCIETAL NORMS

A month or so later, I had the opportunity to use the foundation of these name conversations to launch a new discussion thread that I thought would both interest and challenge my students. Always wanting to make connections clear, I told them, "You might remember, earlier this year, we talked about our names. We explored where they came from and what they mean to us. And we noticed that even when people might have the same first or last name, they have their own stories and meanings for it. We know that someone's name is just one part of who they are. We're going to read a book today about another piece of who we are."

Shades of People, by Shelley Rotner and Sheila M. Kelly, is a beautiful picture book full of photographs of children, mostly close-up photos of their faces. There are pictures of individual children and of children playing together. There are a few adults in the photos with the children. The book begins, "Have you noticed that people come in many different shades? Not colors, exactly, but shades. There's creamy, ivory, sandy and peach, coffee, cocoa, copper and tan." It continues, offering more names for shades, and explaining that "skin is just our covering, like wrapping paper."

I read about half of the book to the class, stopping before the above quote, and then paused. "What do you think about the kids in this book?" I asked. Purposefully beginning the conversation in a way that is open-ended makes space for every student to contribute and also allows me to see where students would naturally take the conversation if encouraged to follow their own interests.

Students quickly began sharing some thoughts:

- "The kids look really happy in this book."

- "That kid is missing his front tooth, just like me!"

- "That boy is wearing glasses. I wear glasses!"

- "Those girls are reading a book together."

- "That kid has freckles. My friend on the bus has a lot of freckles."

- "I have a tie-dye shirt like that one!"

And we did get some thoughts about skin color. (Although the book makes the distinction between colors and shades, my students did not.)

- "His skin color is white, like mine."

- "Those girls (the ones reading the book together) have different skin colors."

- "The kids in this book are lots of different colors."

One conversation took off a bit:

"Her hair has lots of curls, like my hair," said Khadra.

"Yeah! I have hair like that too! My mom usually braids it, though. See?" responded Yaneidy. The two girls compared their hair with the young Black girl in the book. Their classmates followed their lead and began looking for kids in the book who had hair like theirs.

I was a bit surprised that the conversation hadn't touched on the names of the different shades mentioned in the book, but I opted to continue reading the book and return to that topic later. As I finished reading, I came to realize that the students were *far* more fascinated by the pictures than they were by the text. This wasn't completely surprising, but it did make me decide to reimagine my planned conversation. In Chapter 2, we described the difference between showing *agility* and showing *flexibility* in the face of unexpected student comments. (I shared the example of my students' fixation with George Washington's teeth, which led them to the important realization that these teeth probably had been taken from enslaved people.) Here, *agility*—tabling my planned prompts to follow student interest—seemed to be the right move. Originally, I had thought we would discuss various names for the colors of our skin on this day, but as the students were so engrossed with the photographs, I thought our later conversation would benefit from more time spent following that interest.

When we finished the book, I asked students to turn and talk with a partner about the kids in the book. There were many more connections between themselves and the way the kids looked, what they were wearing, and what they were doing. After giving them plenty of time to share these connections, I told students that I would put the book with our other read-alouds (in a display by the carpet) so that they could peruse it at will in the future. I decided to let their natural curiosity and inclination to find connections inspire a future skin color conversation, rather than forcing it in that moment. So I shelved our conversation for a few days. But in the meantime, students *did* pick up the book again and again. They spent full minutes looking closely at each page, talking with friends about what was happening and what it reminded them of or how they connected to it.

RETURNING TO OUR CONVERSATION

Later in the week, I read the book to the class again. This time, I paused more frequently. With each color name, I stopped, and we looked at the picture of the child that went with it. I asked students if they thought the name the authors chose was a good description of the shade of that child's skin. As will be seen in the conversations with middle- and upper-elementary students in Chapters 5 and 6, it can be beneficial to encourage students to question authority figures—authors of books and websites, for example. Students will develop stronger critical thinking skills when their teacher encourages them to be analytical in places where they might be instinctively unquestioning. Overwhelmingly, my students were in agreement with the authors' choices of skin color descriptions in *Shades of People*. We did pause a few times to do a quick online search for a specific color, like ivory, copper, and almond, because students weren't certain what those colors looked like.

FIGURE 4.3
Color words kindergartners used to describe their skin

Then I asked students, "How would you describe the shade of your skin? What words might you use to tell someone who couldn't see you?" I told them to turn and talk with a partner about this question. Students quickly twisted their bodies on the carpet, faced a classmate, and began throwing out ideas. As I hovered around the carpet, I noticed most of the discussions fell into two categories:

1. Students used the words from *Shades of People* to describe themselves.

2. Students used standard color names, like white or brown or black, to describe themselves.

This was about what I had expected would happen. Students were looking closely at their hands and comparing the shade with their partner. When I asked them to turn back to the main group, I was ready to chart their thoughts. We made a list of the words they used to describe the shades of their skin.

Then I asked them, "When you draw a person in art class, what color crayon do you use?" I offered them the choice to go and pick a crayon from one of our tables to share. This gave them a chance to move during our conversation, which I hoped would extend their stamina for it. The physical crayons would also provide a more concrete way to talk about these colors. Most of the students quickly hopped up and hurried to different tables around our classroom. As they rummaged through our crayons, there was a lot of talk.

- "I need to find a brown crayon."
- "Where is that pinkish crayon?"
- "I don't know. None of these crayons look right."

Some students were back on the carpet, crayon in hand, quickly. Others still hovered over crayon tubs with wrinkled brows. I called students to return, saying, "It's okay if you don't have a crayon in your hand. You can describe what you were looking for or you can find a friend who might have the color you wanted." Students worked their way back to the carpet, some more willingly than others.

As they sat back down, I asked, "Look around at the crayons your friends brought to the carpet. Does anyone have the same color as anyone else?" Heads turned right and left as students scanned the crayons they could see.

"Yes, they do!" said Gladis. "I see the same crayons. Khadra has the same color I have!" Khadra looked down at her crayon, comparing it to the one Gladis was holding. "We do have the same one!" she said, excitedly. Yaneidy held up her crayon. It was the same color too.

As they continued to look around, students noticed that Wyatt, Cindy, and Sophia all held the same color crayons. I asked students if there was a name on the paper on their crayon (assuming their crayon still had paper on it, of course). Sophia showed me her crayon. It said pink on the side. Yaneidy brought hers over to me to point out where it said brown. I added pink to our chart of names of shades, and we noted that brown was already on it.

> Khadra, who was standing, spoke up first. "I picked this crayon, but it isn't the same color as my skin."

Then I asked all of the students who were holding brown crayons or who had been looking for a brown crayon to stand up. About a third of our class stood up. I said, "Let's look at all of these friends. They were looking for or have brown crayons for drawing people. Do you think everyone who is standing has skin that is a shade that matches the brown crayon?"

My students looked back and forth at the crayons and at their classmates. Khadra, who was standing, spoke up first. "I picked this crayon, but it isn't the same color as my skin."

I asked her, "What made you pick that crayon?"

"It is the one I use to draw people," she replied.

As that had been the prompt ("When you draw a person in art class, what color crayon do you use?") I had used, Khadra's response made total sense. I had chosen that question because I wanted to make it less personal than it would have been if I had asked them to pick a crayon that matched their skin. By making the question not about their skin but about their activities in art, I had hoped to give them more freedom and less pressure. Now, however, I wanted to steer our conversation in a slightly personal direction.

I asked Khadra, "Is that the crayon you use when you draw yourself?"

"Yeah," she answered.

"You use it, even though it doesn't really match your skin?" I asked.

"Well, yeah," she responded, with a tad more hesitation.

"Thank you, Khadra. That's really helpful for us to know," I told her. Then, turning to the rest of the class, I asked, "How many of you draw yourselves with a crayon that doesn't really match your skin?" Some hands went up quickly. Others took a moment to think about my question, but eventually, everyone had their hand raised. "That's really interesting," I said. "I don't think there's a crayon that really matches my skin either. I usually choose the pink or the peach, if there is one. We saw in *Shades of People* that there are so many different shades that skin can be. It would be hard to have crayons for every shade!"

In hindsight, I regret not asking Khadra more about her decision. Instead of asking her why she chose a color that doesn't really match her skin, I explained why I would choose one that doesn't match my skin. I took over the conversation rather than allowing the students to move it forward.

I went on to ask, "Do you think anyone here is the exact same shade as another friend?" Again, heads turned as everyone looked around at each other. They identified students with very similar skin. But the consensus was that, actually, all of us in our room were different shades. "Wow. We're all totally unique, aren't we?" I asked. "That means we're all different from each other. We're each super special.

"There's a girl, not much older than you, who thought everyone should have a crayon to match their skin." I said. "Do you think she could make crayons for everyone's skin?"

Immediately my students laughed and called out no. "There's too many!" David said.

"Yeah," added Wyatt. "We're all different, so we all need different crayons. That many crayons wouldn't fit in a box!"

A PEER AS A SOURCE

"Well," I told them, "I want to tell you a little more about this girl, and you can see what you think about what she did." I showed them a short video of Bellen Woodard talking about what made her decide to create her own line of crayons and colored pencils. Bellen describes a friend asking her for a "skin-colored crayon." She goes on to say, "I kind of knew what he was referring to, because we kind of named the peach crayon the skin-colored crayon, so I kind of just handed it over" (Tocco 2020). She decided that in the future, if someone asked her for a skin-colored crayon, she was going to "ask them which one, because there could be a number of any beautiful colors" to match someone's skin (Tocco 2020). She says that her company, More Than Peach, is about giving kids "options that actually match them and represent them" (Tocco 2020).

An article and short video interview with Bellen Woodard in which she talks about creating her own line of skin-colored crayons and colored pencils

We watched the video twice. It is short, and young students notice new things each time we watch a video, so I frequently opt to watch things at least twice. Then, after starting the video for a third time, I paused it to allow for some conversation after Bellen tells the story of the "skin-colored crayon" in her classroom. I asked students what they were thinking. "If someone asked you for the 'skin-colored' crayon, would you think the way that Bellen did—would you just know that they meant the peach one?"

The students thought about that for a minute. "Yeah, I think that's what I would guess they wanted," answered Gladis. She sounded a bit hesitant, though, as if she was still thinking about that question.

Wyatt nodded at her. "Uh huh, I would too." A few more students were nodding and murmuring their agreement. Others still looked a little uncertain.

With my next prompt, I tried a slightly different phrasing. "How many of you would pick up a white or pinkish crayon if someone asked you for a 'skin-colored' crayon? Or at least, who thinks they would have done that before we heard Bellen's story? I think that's probably what I would have done before hearing her." I was a little worried that putting myself into this conversation in this way would lead students, but I also wanted them to know that it was okay if they thought that's what they would have done.

Later, as I reflected on our conversation, I wished I had made that question less pointed. I could have asked, "What crayon would you pick up if someone asked you for a 'skin-colored' crayon?" That would have offered students more leeway in their thinking than just asking them an essentially yes/no question.

In response to my pointed question, more than half of the students raised their hands. I looked around at them and asked, "How many of you would use a white or pinkish crayon to draw yourself?" A bunch of hands went down.

"That's really interesting, isn't it?" I asked. "Some of you would pick up that white or pinkish crayon if someone asked you for a 'skin-colored' one, but you wouldn't use that to draw your own skin. Why do you think so many of us see the white or pinkish crayons as the color for drawing people?"

I knew that was a really big question and that we weren't likely to answer it immediately. There was a lot to unpack with this question. I decided we would spend a short time talking about it right then and come back to it with more evidence and prompting. In that moment, students weren't sure about the question. Sophie said, "I think it's 'cause . . . well, we use it because it's what we use."

I nodded and asked, "Are you saying that you think of that crayon as the skin-colored one because that's what you have known it to be?" When she nodded, I asked, "What do you all think about Sophie's idea? Do you agree or disagree?" This phrasing was purposeful (as we mention in Chapter 3). When possible—and *especially* when we might be creating space for a debate—it's important to center a student's *idea* as the thing being critiqued. ("What do you think about Sophie's idea?" versus "Do you think Sophie is wrong or right?")

Her classmates agreed with her idea. Franklin said, "Yeah, that's the one we all know is the skin-color one."

Again, I nodded and said, "It sounds like you feel like Bellen did. That everyone knows that when we say 'skin-colored crayon,' we mean the peach or pinkish or white one. That's really interesting, since a lot of us wouldn't use that crayon to draw ourselves. We're going to explore that a little more soon."

Wrapping up a conversation that isn't really ending, like this one, is a bit of a challenge. My goal here was to stop them for this day, as we'd been talking for a while, but not abruptly. As noted in Chapter 2, it is important to be thoughtful about how we exit conversations, even if it is just for that day and we'll be returning to the topic. One option is to offer students a quick check: "What questions or thoughts do you have that you want to share before we move on to our next activity?" We can also keep an eye on students as they move away from the conversation. Does anyone look confused or uncertain or upset? It is easy in an elementary school day to get caught up in what is coming next, or to feel rushed when students start losing stamina for a conversation. When this happens, we might be tempted to cut short the ending. But ending discussions thoughtfully is something I have learned to be conscious of because of its importance in ensuring our students continue to feel comfortable in our conversations.

WHAT MAKES WHITE THE DEFAULT?

A couple of days later we returned to our conversation about crayons and skin color, ready to use what we'd previously discussed to ask a big question and, hopefully, inspire new thinking. To start, I reviewed our earlier conversation: "We've read *Shades of People*; some of you have read it many times by now! And we have thought about how our skin can be lots of different shades. Then we learned about Bellen Woodard and her company, More Than Peach, which makes crayons in lots of shades to match people's skin. We noticed that a lot of us think of the peach or pinkish or white crayons as the ones for drawing people, even though we wouldn't always use those crayons to draw ourselves. We were wondering why that might be true. Why would people assume those colors are the 'right' colors for drawing people?"

I continued: "Today we're going to explore some possibilities for why that might be. We're going to work in groups to see what we can find in different areas. One group is going to look at the books in our classroom library. Another group is going to look at these magazines. And another group is going to look at the websites we use a lot. In your group, you are going to look at the people you see. Not the people in your group, but the people in the books or magazines or on the websites. You're going to think about this question: *What crayon would I use to draw those people?*"

I divided the class into three small groups. (We described this strategy, along with the strategy of pairing students up with partners, in Chapter 3.)

Forming small groups often requires a bit more work than having students turn to a partner. It can take a bit longer for students to be ready, but it allows them to engage in a conversation with a wider breadth of ideas. Having more students in a group means each student will have less time to talk, but it also means they'll hear the thinking of more than one other person. There are times when partner talk is needed to give every student an opportunity to get their ideas out there. At other times, like this one, it can be helpful for students to have more brains sharing ideas to keep the conversation flowing.

I sent one group off to our classroom library and then got another group settled at a table with a stack of magazines. I had gathered kids' magazines, like *Highlights*, *Sports Illustrated for Kids*, and *National Geographic Kids*, as well as some magazines for older audiences, like *Good Housekeeping*. I wanted to have a range of photos without worrying about swimsuit photos or alcohol ads (things that would likely distract students, who would want to tell me how inappropriate they were).

I had the last group sit down at a table with several laptops, two students per laptop. On each laptop I had a different website open. I included myON, a site full of books, PBS Kids, and Sesame Street. My students were used to using these sites, so I felt confident they could navigate them pretty independently. Once they were up and rolling, I began moving among the groups.

I would pop over to a group and ask them how they were doing and what they were noticing. All of the groups were finding diverse people represented in the books, magazines, and websites. They showed me lots of people who would not be well represented by the peach crayon. I had expected that to be true, for a couple of different reasons. In our classroom library, I work hard to ensure we have books that reflect lots of different people in lots of different ways. In the magazines and websites, I think there is a conscious and concerted effort to be more diverse than in the past. All of that is wonderful, and I was thrilled my students got to see that.

However, overall, in our classroom library, in the magazines, and on the websites, there are still more White people (and characters) than there are people (or characters) of color, and my students didn't seem to be noticing that. I should have anticipated, after all of our discussions about skin color, that they would be focused on the diversity of color and *not* on the ratios of those colors. I had not, so I had to find a way to remedy that.

After giving students a little bit of time to explore with their group, I pulled them back together. I suggested that it might be worth collecting some data about what they were noticing. I grabbed a basket from our classroom library and modeled what I was thinking.

At the top of a piece of paper I wrote "Yes" and "No." I explained that *Yes* meant "Yes, that character or person could use the peach crayon to draw themselves," and *No* meant that they would not likely use the peach crayon. I picked up the first book in the basket and looked at the cover. It was *The Teacher from the Black Lagoon* by Mike Thaler. I pointed at the boy on the cover and said, "I think he would use the peach crayon, so I'm going to put a mark under *Yes*." The next book I pulled out was *The Day You Begin* by Jacqueline Woodson. This time I said, "I don't think she would use the peach crayon, so this time I'll put a mark under *No*." I did this with a few more books, asking my students where I should put the mark. Then I sent them back off with their groups and some paper.

As they collected and recorded their data, there was some surprise. The groups were finding they were making more marks under *Yes* than they were under *No*. After a bit, I asked students to return to the carpet with their papers. As they came back to our circle, they were already looking at each other's papers and talking about what they noticed. As a result, I decided to give them some time to talk in small groups.

I made groups with one student from each of the three previous groups (classroom library, magazines, websites). I explained to them, "In your group you have one person who looked at our classroom library, one person who looked at magazines, and one person who looked at websites. You can share what your group found and listen to your friends share about the other groups. Then you can see what was the same and what was different about what your groups noticed."

As I listened to these small-group discussions, I heard many students exclaiming in surprise that each group had more marks for *Yes* than for *No*. Some groups noticed that the website data were the closest for yeses and nos. Some groups counted all of the marks. Some students shared examples of what they had found, describing book covers or magazine articles or websites. They probably could have talked for quite some time, but I pulled them back to the whole group after about five minutes. I wanted us to have a strong discussion all together, and I didn't want them to use up all of their stamina in their small groups.

With the whole group I asked, "So, what did you notice when you shared your data?" The first few students said things like this:

- Our group had nine marks under *Yes* and four marks under *No*.

- We saw lots of kids when we looked. There weren't a lot of adults.

- We had more marks on our paper than the other groups.

Yaneidy said, "All of us had more marks for *Yes* than for *No*."
I looked at her with wide eyes and asked, "All of you did?"
She nodded vigorously at me. "Yes. All of us did."
With my eyes still wide, I slowly scanned the rest of the group. "What about you all? Did you all find the same thing that Yaneidy's group found?"

Heads nodded all around the group. Students called out "Yes!" and "We did!" I continued gaping at them as if I found this completely shocking. They nodded and nodded, as if they felt they needed to convince me.

"Okay," I said slowly, as if I were thinking something through. "You all noticed that there are more people in our books, magazines, and websites who *would* probably use the peach crayon than there are ones who would not probably use it. Is that what you are telling me?" Heads nodded vigorously again.

"Well." I said and paused. "Well. What do you think that means for our earlier conversation? Does that give you any ideas about why so many people assume that when someone says 'skin-colored crayon,' they mean the peach one?"

The students thought for a moment and then David said, "Because there are so many people who would use it?"

I noticed the way he phrased the idea as a question and said, "That's interesting, David. Thank you for sharing that idea."

Khadra agreed with him. "Yeah, if lots of people use it, that's what we think of." Other heads around the circle began nodding.

"Okay," I said. "I can see what you mean. You noticed that there were a lot of people who would use the peach crayon. So what do you think about Bellen's crayons? Do you think we should just think of the peach crayon as the skin-colored one, or do you think we need to have more choices?"

"We need more choices!" stated Khadra.

"I think Bellen is right."

"Yeah," added Franklin, "lots of people don't want to use the peach crayon. They should get colors that they want."

Quickly students were adding on and agreeing with Khadra and Franklin. There was a clear consensus that Bellen Woodard was right and kids should have crayons that represent them.

To wrap up our conversation, I asked students to look at our list of words to describe skin shades. "If you were going to design a new set of crayons for drawing people and you could put eight in a box, which colors would you want to include?" Students turned to discuss with a partner which shades would be the best to have.

FINAL REFLECTION

We didn't get quite where I had thought we might in this conversation. Students recognized that there were more White folks represented in media than there were people of color, but their read was that there are more White folks than people of color, period. They were not seeing that representation in media might not match reality.

> I did not have to get to everything, much less "change the world" with any one conversation.

I made the decision to wrap up this conversation for now without getting to that point. On reflection, I wish I had gone just a bit farther. I could have asked my students what crayon colors would be most used in our class. Our classroom (and school) was majority people of color. My students might (and I'll never know now) have been able to take their thinking a little farther if they had considered the data they had collected in comparison with our classroom and school. (That is obviously not true everywhere, but it could have been an interesting addition to our conversation.)

At the time, I felt that these young students had become more aware of and able to notice representation, even if they were not yet extrapolating about that representation. They were also beginning to think about the ways we talk and think about race, often without noticing it.

No conversation will stand on its own. I knew that this skin color conversation—like the name conversation before it—was just another building block for many similar race conversations planned for the year. I did not have to get to everything, much less "change the world" with any one conversation. Nor do you. Each well-planned race conversation makes us all a little better, especially when we have made our early-elementary classrooms places that celebrate growth.

CHAPTER 5

HOW THE PAST IMPACTS THE PRESENT IN MIDDLE ELEMENTARY

As we noted in Chapter 2, knowing your standards well is important when engaging in race conversations. Many state standards for various grade levels, including middle-elementary grades, address discussions about how the past impacts the present. For units about ancient civilizations, for example, the standards often focus on inventions from those past cultures—like fireworks and written language—that we still use today. It can be powerful for kids to see that creations from millennia before their births are still common.

From another perspective, however, to focus on inventions is to engage in a pretty surface exploration of the complex ways that the past impacts us now. This is especially true when it comes to understanding how this country's racial history—including the role played by racist ideas—has impacted our lives. If elementary students never discuss how past actions, court decisions, legislation, and more still play a large role in how our society *currently* functions, they will not be prepared to richly discuss current inequities, both now and in their later academic lives. Conversely, if we make the chronology and the impact of racial events clear, students will be more likely to develop analytical and critical lenses that help them to authentically understand both the past and the present.

The classroom conversations we explore in this chapter were about U.S. history and were geared for middle-elementary (second- and third-grade) students. I've personally led versions of this chapter's conversations with third graders a number of times. Full disclosure: these discussions might be less successful with second graders until later in the school year. They would probably work well with fourth or fifth graders, though. That said, you are the one who knows your students, and you will best be able to decide what conversations will work well for them and when they would be the most effective.

CONNECTING TO THE STANDARDS
GRADE 3 ENGLISH STANDARDS

3.1 The student will use effective communication skills in a variety of settings.

   c) Ask and respond to questions from teachers and other group members.

   d) Orally summarize information expressing ideas clearly.

3.5 The student will read and demonstrate comprehension of fictional texts, literary nonfiction, and poetry.

   b) Make connections between reading selections.

   g) Ask and answer questions about what is read.

   h) Draw conclusions using the text for support.

3.6 The student will continue to read and demonstrate comprehension of nonfiction texts.

   a) Identify the author's purpose.

   b) Use prior and background knowledge as context for new learning.

   d) Ask and answer questions about what is read using the text for support.

   e) Draw conclusions using the text for support.

(Virginia Department of Education 2017, 15–16)

**GRADE 3 HISTORY AND
SOCIAL STUDIES STANDARDS**

3.1 The student will demonstrate skills for historical thinking,
geographical analysis, economic decision making, and
responsible citizenship by

d) summarizing points and evidence to answer a question;

f) determining relationships with multiple causes
or effects;

g) explaining connections across time and place;

(Virginia Department of Education 2015, 1)

CONSTITUTION DAY

In 2004, Senator Robert Byrd amended that year's omnibus spending
bill with a requirement that any educational institution that receives
federal money must provide teaching about the United States Constitution on September 17, the anniversary of the signing of that document.
September 17 is fairly early in the school year in most districts across the
country. That makes it a prime time to begin yearlong discussions of how
our country's origins impact
the way it continues to function
today, more than two hundred
years later.

On a typical Constitution
Day, I begin with a very general
morning message for my third
graders. In Figure 5.1, you can

> I prefer to begin conversations
> with more open-ended prompts,
> like "What thoughts do you
> have about that?" (or frequently,
> "What do you notice? What do
> you wonder?").

see this message (as well as some of the notations made after the start of
our conversation). With middle- and upper-elementary students, I prefer to begin conversations with more open-ended prompts, like "What
thoughts do you have about that?" (or frequently, "What do you notice?
What do you wonder?").

Starting with a broader question does two things:

1. It offers a low floor. Any student can step in and share what they're thinking, because it is clear there is not one single right answer. This gives students more options for participating in the conversation right away.

2. It serves as a quick, informal preassessment for me, giving me some idea of what my students are bringing to this conversation in this moment.

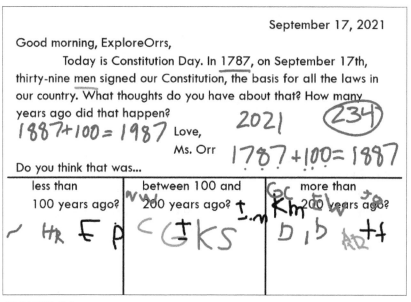

FIGURE 5.1
Jen's Morning Message to her class on Constitution Day

Before any of the notations were made on this board, students had the opportunity to share their thoughts with the whole class. Some shared that 1787 seemed like a long time ago, so we paused to work together to figure out that it was more than two hundred years ago (Figure 5.1). That revelation caused some gasps as everyone realized how long ago this was. Timothy then said, "Thirty-nine *men*? Only *men* signed it?" Others, who hadn't yet processed that bit, chimed in supporting that question, wondering how that was possible.

FIGURE 5.2
An image of the signers of the United States Constitution

This was my cue to pull up an image showing the signers of the Constitution. I explained, just in case they hadn't been paying attention to the title, that these were the men who had signed it more than two hundred years ago. Immediately there were some snickers and whispered comments to classmates about the clothing and the hair. I gave students a bit of time to note how these men looked different from what we might expect today, knowing that's what they were going to talk about first regardless of what I did!

Student interests in the conversation

It's important that we give time and space for our students to engage their initial interests. For one thing, if they don't get the chance to talk through the things that have caught their attention, they are likely to remain focused on them and be less able (or willing) to follow any direction I give with my prompts. This is a lesson I learned through the error of not giving students time—at this specific moment—in previous years. Secondly, allowing time and space communicates that their ideas are valid, even if I am going to root our conversation in *different* observations. Their seemingly unrelated observations might even organically lead us right into our agenda or, even better, highlight a worthwhile discussion path that hadn't occurred to me!

After giving students a few moments to study the image of the signers of the Constitution, I asked them to turn and talk with a partner about what they saw. *What do they notice? What do they wonder?*

The room buzzed with their conversations.

- I notice that they look really funny!

- What are they wearing? Why do all of their shirts go way up their necks?

- Is that their real hair? Why do so many of them have long hair?

- I notice that a few of them are smiling but most of them aren't. They look really serious.

I roamed around, listening in here and there. When I was nearby, students asked me questions about what they were wondering, and I responded with versions of "That's a great question. You should share that when we return to the whole group." My goal, as they spoke with their partners, was not that they would get answers, but that they would look critically at the image and be prepared to participate energetically in what would be a complex conversation.

When we turned back to the whole group, some students shared that they had spotted George Washington in the picture and wanted to confirm that he had signed the Constitution. By third grade, students typically know Washington as our first president but often know very little else about him. They wondered if other presidents had signed, and I pointed out James Madison, another Virginian and our fourth president.

At this point, Kennedy raised her hand and said, "They're all White." Again, those students who hadn't yet noted this gasped and looked at each other, as if to confirm the accuracy of Kennedy's statement. I didn't say anything for a moment, giving them time to look closely at the image and check for themselves. Some students talked with nearby classmates, discussing whether a specific person was White or not. The idea that every member of this august group was White was clearly almost unbelievable for them.

After a moment, I did confirm Kennedy's observation and added another piece of information. I explained that in 1787, only men could vote and, more specifically, only men who owned land. This meant that only wealthy White men could vote. Again, I stopped and gave students time to talk to a partner about their thinking.

More benefits of partner talk

For eight-year-olds, the idea that our country functioned so differently in its early years is shocking. These kids were born during Obama's presidency. I had a third grader tell me that he voted for Hillary Clinton in 2016 (and I love that he said *he* voted) because, he said, "it's been a long time since we had a girl president." He was shocked when I told him we'd *never* had a female president. Young children's view of the world is shaped by what they have seen and experienced. History, even just a few years back, can be difficult for them to

> Young children's view of the world is shaped by what they have seen and experienced.

comprehend. Partner talk—as a conversational structure—makes a lot of sense in this situation. Unlike whole-class conversation, partner talk gives every student the time to share their thoughts. In addition to this benefit, there is also the intimacy of partner talk. Without an audience of classmates to critique their comments, students can somewhat confidentially work through their understanding as they take on surprising new ideas.

As the children spoke with partners, I eavesdropped on Lila and Elias.

Elias: *Why would they have only allowed some people to vote? What was their problem?*

Lila: *I know, right? That's not fair at all.*

As they talked, they both realized they would not have been allowed to vote, since Lila was female and Elias was Black. They got angry, their sense that people like them were not valued in the early years of our country causing them to quietly fume. They weren't alone. When we returned to the whole group, the prevailing feeling was one of anger, and the majority of the comments were full of frustration and confusion. Many of my young students were suddenly realizing they couldn't see themselves in the early history of our country.

After giving them a few minutes to vent their frustration, because it can be tough to think analytically when you're focused on your anger, I asked Elias's question to the whole class, crediting him with it. "Elias asked a good question. Why would the founders of our country have only wanted *some* people to have a voice in our government?" I had thought that, with some guidance, we'd get to a discussion of who was able to get an education, but Gabby suggested that the founders just didn't like people who were different.

Others nodded agreement, and Dylan chimed in, "Even today some people don't like people who are different."

I hadn't anticipated that, but I wanted to highlight this connection between the past and present. I paused the sharing to say, "Dylan, that's really interesting. We've been talking so much about how different things were more than two hundred years ago. We noticed they wore different clothes and had different hair styles, and we learned that many people didn't have rights then that they have now. You've noticed that, in spite of all of those differences, there are things that are the same now as they were then." Dylan nodded sagely. Others looked at him in awe. It was silent for a moment as students considered this possibility, that there were things that were the same now as they had been in a time that had seemed quite foreign to them throughout this conversation.

In that moment, I added one more piece of information. "Dylan's observation is very astute. Some things are the same now as they were then. I want to tell you about one thing that has changed. All of these thirty-nine men were landowners, which meant they were fairly wealthy for their time. Many of them also owned enslaved people. Both George Washington and James Madison, men who would later become president, were slave owners."

In the shocked silence that followed that statement, Kennedy couldn't restrain herself. She blurted loudly, "Well that's just rude!" Others agreed, verbally and by nodding their heads vigorously.

Then I asked them the question that would guide our conversations for quite some time. I said, "What do you think it means for us, right now, to live in a country that was created only by wealthy White men? How do you think we are impacted by the fact that only wealthy White men had a voice in the formation of this country?" My question was met with silence, which was what I had anticipated. It's a big question no matter how old you are.

I suggested to my students that they think some about that question, maybe even talk to family or friends about it, if they wished, and that we would come back to it again. I assured them that we would be talking about this big question throughout the year, and making sense of it together.

THE EMANCIPATION PROCLAMATION

A few days after the anniversary of the signing of the Constitution, we reach the anniversary of the Emancipation Proclamation. Elementary students, even our youngest ones, usually have some knowledge of the history of slavery in this country. However, understanding what the Emancipation Proclamation was and what it did is very complicated. I don't think I fully understood it until I was an adult (and maybe I still don't, as much as I think I do). So it's a tricky bit of history to engage in with young children. However, the change from slavery being *legal* to *illegal* is definitely one young children can understand.

Writing to organize student thinking

To kick off our conversation about the Emancipation Proclamation, I asked my third-grade students to take a few minutes to write down some thinking. This orientation allows students to pause before they jump into a big conversation, while also encouraging them to get their ideas organized. I told them, "Seventy-five years and five days after those thirty-nine men signed the Constitution, President Lincoln signed another document, the Emancipation Proclamation. That document freed the enslaved people here in Virginia."

I recognize that this isn't the full story of the Emancipation Proclamation. In fact, to be truly historically accurate, Lincoln's signing the Emancipation Proclamation did nothing for enslaved people in Virginia at that time, as slave owners in Virginia felt no need to abide by anything

Lincoln made law. Virginia had seceded from, and was rebelling against, the United States, so Virginians did not believe they were bound by US law. However, considering that there are many adults who do not fully understand the Emancipation Proclamation and what it did and did not do (at least immediately), it seems unrealistic to expect third graders to grasp the entire story in one discussion. Trying to explain the fully accurate history would mean a significant detour away from our conversation. So, in that moment, I opted to keep to some basics *and* keep us focused on Virginia to increase the relevance for my students.

I offered students three broad prompts to choose from, both verbally and visually, projected on the board:

1. What do you think might have changed in those 75 years that led to Lincoln freeing enslaved people?

2. What kind of responses do you think there were to the Emancipation Proclamation? How might different people have responded differently?

3. This happened 160 years ago. What has changed, since then, in what it means to be Black in the United States?

Most students started writing immediately. I hoped that even though this was relatively early in the year, the community-building work and purposeful pedagogy described in Part 1 of this book had shown my students that their developing ideas were valued, and it wasn't about needing to be right. From day one, we had pointed out student mistakes without judgment, and even with celebrations. They hopefully knew our focus was on sharing our thinking, asking questions, and learning together. But even with all of this, a few students definitely looked a bit lost or stumped by the prompt as their classmates grabbed pens and got going. I tried to kneel down next to as many of them as possible and see if there was any way I could help. Most of the time, students needed clarification. My wording wasn't super kid friendly, a choice I had made deliberately. I had no intention of oversimplifying this discussion because I underestimated my students. Underestimating my students is something I work to remain vigilant about because it is easy to slip up. I would rather talk through a question with a child (or children) and tease out its meaning together than have them not think as deeply as they could because I didn't set them up well.

Pivoting to one-on-one *teacher* talk

Earlier in this chapter's Constitution Day conversation, I described the importance and application of the one-on-one partner talk we introduced in Chapter 3. Now, in this conversation about the Emancipation Proclamation, my students instead benefitted from one-on-one exchanges *with me*. In an intimate setting, teachers can clarify and supplement the language of particularly challenging prompts.

I crouched down next to Amina and asked if she wanted to talk about her thinking. She said, "Ms. Orr, I don't understand what you're asking."

"No worries," I told her. "Let's talk about the questions and see what you think." I read the first question to her and asked what she was thinking. Some of my third graders may still have trouble with their decoding skills, and if I read a question aloud to them, allowing them to just focus on the meaning of it, they often are good to go. Amina still looked perplexed. After pausing for about thirty seconds, to give her time to think and talk, if she was ready, I went on. "We know that back when the Constitution was signed, many people owned enslaved people. It was a normal part of life in this country. When Lincoln was president, about seventy-five years later, he worked to free those enslaved people. What do you think might have *changed*, in our country, for people to be working to change something that *had* been seen as normal? To make such a *big* move?"

Her eyes got big, and I could see she was thinking about this. "I don't know," she said. "Maybe people realized it wasn't right to own people." I suggested she start writing about that and I moved on, noting to myself to make sure she had the opportunity to share in the whole group.

Nala, one of my Black students, was writing furiously but waved me over. She was a positive student who often thought passionately about whatever we were learning. "Ms. Orr, I'm writing about that third question."

"That's great," I responded. "It'll be really interesting for all of us to hear your thoughts on that."

"I have a lot!" she replied. "I've talked to my parents about this and my grandparents." I could see she'd done a lot of writing already and encouraged her to keep at it.

Nicholas seemed to be in a similar place as Amina. I opted to read the second question (*What kind of responses do you think there were to the Emancipation Proclamation? How might different people have responded differently?*) to him and to start there. After I read it, he asked, "What do you mean by 'different people'?"

"Well," I responded, "are there some people who might have been really happy for Lincoln to do this? Who might have wanted this to happen?" He paused for a moment, reflecting on the question before answering.

"Slaves would have been happy to not be slaves anymore."

"Yeah, I agree with you about that. Who might have felt differently? Who might *not* have been happy?" While Nicholas thought about that, I left him to his writing and continued moving about the room.

Of course, there were a couple of students who said to me, "Ms. Orr, I have no idea what to write. I don't know anything about this." My response to them was that it was okay to not be prepared to answer these questions—they were big questions. Maybe, after listening to their classmates, they would feel differently. I reminded them that that was why we had conversations in our classroom, so we could learn from each other.

A NOTE ON LANGUAGE

Throughout this conversation, my students regularly used the term *slaves*, and I did not correct them. *I* regularly used the term *enslaved people*, but I didn't draw attention to it. I modeled better language for them but saved the explicit discussion about why one option might be more respectful than another for a future time. My students had heard the word slaves for many years. They were less likely to be familiar with the term enslaved people. This language shift is a big conversation to have, and one that deserves to be had *well*. So I chose to shelve that, in this moment, in order to focus on the conversation at hand.

HOW THE PAST IMPACTS THE PRESENT

Pivoting to whole-class discussion

I had offered students three different questions so that, hopefully, they
would all have something they felt they could offer to the whole class, but
I realized that some might not feel that they did. I also had to decide if we
were going to focus on one question at a time or just jump into the whole-
class discussion with a broader prompt. I opted for just jumping in, with
the backup plan of focusing on
a specific question if it seemed
necessary. When we started our
class discussion, there were a
few students who were primed
and ready to get us going.

> Asking for more information
> can be really important, but it
> isn't always easy. Sometimes
> you might worry you won't look
> very smart or that you'll hurt
> someone's feelings if you don't
> understand.

Not surprisingly, when I
asked if anyone wanted to share,
Nala started us off. "It's a lot bet-
ter now than it was when Black people were slaves. I mean, seriously. But
my mom and dad have told me lots of stories about how it still isn't okay.
Black people are still treated badly." Some of her classmates were nodding
in agreement, while others were looking a bit uncertain.

I turned to one who had a questioning look on his face. "What are you
thinking, Mason? You look like you might have a question."

"Yeah," he said slowly. "I'm not really sure about what Nala said. What
does that mean that some Black people are treated bad?"

Before turning back to Nala, I stopped to say, "Mason, thank you for
sharing that question. We may not always understand each other in our
conversations. Asking for more information can be really important, but
it isn't always easy. Sometimes you might worry you won't look very smart
or that you'll hurt someone's feelings if you don't understand. It's a risk,
and I'm so glad you took that risk right now because I am sure Nala has
more to share." I turned back to Nala.

I should note that even just a few weeks into the school year, I felt
confident Nala would be able and willing to respond to Mason's question.
She had proven herself, in that time, to be confident in her thinking and
open to new ideas and new learning. If I had felt less certain, I would not
have just thrown the conversation back her way; I would have offered her

137

the option to respond or not or to help her formulate her response with some more questions from me. But I didn't think that was necessary here. Fortunately, I was right.

"My dad talks about how often he gets stopped by the police when he's driving, even though he hasn't done anything wrong. My mom complains about how expensive it is to buy stuff for her hair and how it can be hard to find it, especially in some places. It's not as big as slavery or not being allowed to go places, but it's still not right."

Mason didn't look totally certain, but he nodded his gratitude at Nala for her clarification. I thanked her for giving us more information about her initial statement and turned to the rest of class. "Anyone have more questions for Nala or want to add on to what she's saying?" Many of the students looked hesitant. I paused, trying to give them enough wait time to gather their thoughts in order to feel ready to speak up. After some silence, I thought that maybe students were not sure of how to share other thoughts after Nala's very personal start.

So I tried again, pointing to the projection on our board. "Nala shared some thoughts about that third question. [*This happened 160 years ago. What has changed, since then, in what it means to be Black in the United States?*] Did anyone else reflect on or write about that question and want to share?" I try very hard not to force students to share, ever. I will often ask them if they are *willing* to share, but I do all I can to make it clear that they don't *have* to. When students are ready to take the risk of speaking up—and it is definitely a risk—they will. If they aren't ready and I force them, it is likely to mean they will not want to share again and will lose some trust in me. My wording here was deliberate. I did not just ask if anyone had focused on that question, because that would have implied that someone needed to speak. My addition of "and want to share" was intended to communicate that the choice was theirs.

It remained quiet. I waited about a minute, biting my tongue—because, like many of us, I'm not great at waiting patiently—before saying, "Okay, how about one of the other questions? Does anyone want to share thoughts on one of those?"

Fatmata, a student whose mother had immigrated from western Africa, raised her hand. "I was thinking about that second question. [*What kind of responses do you think there were to the Emancipation Proclamation? How might different people have responded differently?*] If I had been alive then, I would have been glad Lincoln did that. I might have been a slave, so I would have wanted that to stop."

I noticed Nicholas nodding, as well as other classmates. I waited to be sure that Fatmata was finished and then said, "Thank you, Fatmata, for keeping our conversation going, and for sharing your thinking and why you came to that. Anyone want to add on?"

Aidan raised his hand. "My parents took me to visit Mount, um, that place where George Washington lived."

I helped him out. "Mount Vernon?"

"Yeah, that!" he said. Our school is just a few miles from Mount Vernon, so some students had visited. Aidan continued. "They told us about the people who lived there who were slaves. There were a lot of them, and they did a lot of the work. If George Washington hadn't had those slaves, who would have done all that work? I think he wouldn't have wanted Lincoln to free them."

I could see a few faces get a bit stormy at this statement, and I wondered if they thought that Aidan was defending slavery. I saw some hands go up, but I waited a moment, this time for myself. I wanted to be sure everyone felt like they had a voice in this conversation, so I debated what my next step should be. Should I call on another student and see where they took it? Should I ask Aidan a clarifying question? Should I share my own opinion about what was just said? Did I trust my students, and myself, to be able to continue this conversation in a way that made space for everyone's voice and in which everyone truly listened to each other? Remember, this conversation took place in September. Later in the school year, this would be a much easier moment to navigate, as we would have had more time to develop our community and learn to trust and support each other. In this moment, I decided on trust. I would trust that my students were willing and able to listen to one another carefully and to ask questions to clarify in respectful ways. Even this early in the year, with only a few weeks together, I would trust in the strong community-building work that we had done. And I would trust that I would be able to regain control of the conversation if, by chance, the students were not able to listen and/or clarify.

I called on Nala again.

"I agree with Aidan that George Washington wouldn't have wanted Lincoln to do that if the slaves did all the work for him. But he could have figured out other ways to do it. He didn't have to have slaves!" When Nala saw Aidan nodding in agreement with her, her shoulders relaxed a little bit. Her language was especially impressive to me, because it showed that she had been *listening actively* to Aidan. She had directly cited his words—more or less—and was engaging his idea directly. This is tougher to do when disagreeing or critiquing a classmate. It certainly wasn't the personal attack that the adult world models. As I beamed, other students muttered their agreement, and I heard lots of "No kidding," "Seriously," and, "It's so wrong."

I drew together what Fatmata, Aidan, and Nala had all said: "Thank you all for getting us thinking about who would have supported Lincoln and who would have disagreed or been upset. Enslaved people would have felt differently than slave owners would have. Amina, you and I talked a little bit about that first question [*What do you think might have changed in those 75 years that led to Lincoln freeing enslaved people?*]. Would you be willing to share your thoughts?"

Amina looked down at her paper, took a deep breath, and said, "I think so. I didn't really understand the question, so I'm not sure if I'm right."

I jumped in to say, "Amina, don't worry about that, because there isn't one right or wrong answer to that question. If we look at it, it says 'what do you think,' so whatever you are thinking is what we want to hear."

Amina didn't seem super reassured, but she got started again. "I was thinking that maybe when the Constitution was signed, people thought it was okay to own slaves and then, later, they decided it wasn't."

I gave a moment for students to think before saying, "Amina, it sounds to me like you're saying that one thing that might have changed was how people felt about slavery—that they used to think owning people was okay, and then they didn't think it was okay. Thank you for sharing that thought. Does anyone want to add on or share their thoughts?"

Hannah, who was often quiet during conversations, clearly listening intently but rarely speaking, raised her hand. "I don't get it. How could they have thought it was okay to have slaves? It's not right."

Again, her classmates couldn't hold back their thoughts. There was lots of muttered agreement and comments like "I know, right?" and "It wasn't fair." I stayed quiet and let them process these thoughts and feelings aloud. It's not as if they were only then discovering that they thought slavery was wrong, but for many of them, this was probably the first time they'd stopped to think about it that closely. It was certainly the first time many of them faced the idea that people who are worshiped as heroes, like George Washington, did something so horrific and shocking. I wanted to be sure they had time to really process that.

As they thought about this, they found that they had a lot of questions:

- "How could *anyone* have thought that was okay?"
- "Did *everyone* own slaves when George Washington was president?"
- "Why did the slaves not fight back or run away?"
- "Why did anyone disagree with Lincoln when he wanted to change it?"

Despite this passion, I knew that, at this point, we were getting close to hitting a wall with the attention span and stamina for third graders. Some of these students could and would discuss this all day, but we'd been at it for half an hour, and other students were losing steam. So I opted to focus on one of the three questions as a way to smoothly exit the day's discussion.

"Luis just asked why anyone would have disagreed with Lincoln. You all already talked about how slave owners would have been

> Returning to partner talk meant that each student would have a more active role, sharing their thinking or responding to just one person.

unhappy. They would have had to find other ways to get all of their work done without enslaved people. Who else might have been unhappy with Lincoln's action? Talk with a partner about your ideas." Even as I spoke, the students' loss of stamina was rapidly becoming more apparent. I knew it would be harder for them to focus and listen to the whole group. Returning to partner talk meant that each student would have a more active role, sharing their thinking or responding to just one person. I also knew that when we did return to the whole group, which I believed was important, I was going to have to make the moment quick and meaningful. That meant I had to eavesdrop closely on conversations and, hopefully, overhear some key thoughts that we could focus on for our closing.

As I slowly wandered, listening in to partners, I heard a lot of students feeling very confused by the idea that anyone other than slave owners would have wanted to keep the institution of slavery. That wasn't surprising. My goal, however, was to set us up to talk in the future about a topic that might be similarly confusing: White people's complex responses to Jim Crow laws and the Civil Rights Movement. Luckily, in her partner conversation, Nala was able to connect her thoughts to the third prompt: *This happened 160 years ago. What has changed, since then, in what it means to be Black in the United States?*

In the whole group, I asked Nala and her partner, Tahir, to share what they had been discussing. Nala immediately jumped in: "My parents aren't slaves, but they are still treated badly because they're Black. Sometimes. Some people just don't want Black people to do well. I bet that was the same back then." It's clear that Nala's words were clarifying the thinking of some classmates, while others still seemed to be uncertain about this. Their moral compass could not accept the idea of slavery, and they were unable to make sense of people's acceptance of it.

I thanked my students for all of the thoughtfulness in their questions and their ideas. I told them that if they still had conflicted or confused thoughts about this topic, it was totally reasonable. We were tackling some really big ideas. I told them that some adults still have conflicted or confused thoughts about our nation's past. I let them know that this conversation wasn't over. We would be talking more about how the past has shaped the world we live in. I also let them know that while we were just getting started, their thinking was already helping us understand our world better.

RUBY BRIDGES: MAKING PERSONAL CONNECTIONS

The fall includes other big anniversaries that offer opportunities to link to these early race conversations: September 25, 1957, was the date that the Little Rock Nine began attending Central High School. November 14, 1960, was the date that Ruby Bridges first walked into William Frantz Elementary School in New Orleans, escorted by U.S. Marshals. I decided the exact date wasn't required for this conversation, because I didn't want to wait until November 14 and because the idea of Ruby Bridges entering an all-White school as a first grader was more relatable to my third graders than the Little Rock Nine would be. My students had a memory of entering first grade. They couldn't yet conceive of what entering high school would be like.

One of the challenges of discussing racism with young children is that many of them frequently see it as something in the past and only in the past. Nala's comments in our discussion of the Emancipation Proclamation challenged that, but it remained a difficult concept for many students. I hoped that introducing them to Ruby Bridges, showing them the work she is still doing today, and connecting her experiences to their own would give them a new appreciation of how the past impacts the present.

To begin, I asked students to think back to their first-grade year. For this particular group of students, that year began as any other but ended in the throes of a global pandemic. I had students turn and talk with a partner about their memories from the first day of first grade. *Where did they live? Who was their teacher? What do they remember about their classroom? Their friends?* My goal was for them to get as clear and vivid a picture of that time as possible. I asked a few students to share out in the whole group, both to honor their partner conversations and, hopefully, to stir up more memories for their classmates. Then I asked them to talk with their partners about the beginning of second grade. For many of these students, that year began online. Or it may have begun with everyone wearing masks. It was a different "beginning" than the previous year. I asked students to reflect on how that felt.

As I wandered among the students and listened to conversations, I heard a range of thoughts. Some students remembered how confusing it was to be online all day. Lina mentioned how her younger brother would bother her while she was trying to listen in class. Kaydra agreed. She said her little sister always wanted to be a part of things. She talked about letting her sit with her to listen to stories during reading. Jason said he had just moved before second grade, so he didn't know anyone. He shared how strange it was to have a class full of kids he didn't know and couldn't really talk to. When students shared out to the whole class, there were a lot of connections and nodding heads.

I then explained to students that we were going to learn about someone who had had a very unusual first-grade year. She, like them, had experienced a year of school that was normal—for her it was kindergarten—and then the following year was not normal at all.

The short video that Jen uses to introduce her students to Ruby Bridges (Scholastic 2021)

I showed them a short video about Ruby Bridges from Scholastic. Using primary sources with young children is important and challenging. They are still developing their reading skills, and that makes it difficult to use written texts from the past. Showing students a video makes this history more accessible and clear to them. The Bridges video was short enough to hold their attention, and it showed Ruby Bridges in the present, as an adult, making it easier to see how recent this history was. Young students frequently think everything they learn about history happened very long ago. They do not always have enough perspective to recognize the differences in chronological distance of events. Ruby Bridges's age was a very clear and powerful illustration of how recent the fifties- and sixties-era Civil Rights Movement actually was.

As we watched the video, my students' faces showed a range of emotions: anger, shock, disbelief. I asked them if they wanted to watch it again. I frequently offer students this option. I noticed one day, as I was listening to NPR during my commute, that I hadn't listened carefully to the beginning of a story because it hadn't captured my attention. Then, midway through, it did, but I had missed some crucial context. I would have liked to be able to listen again. It occurred to me that my students might feel similarly. They don't always take me up on the offer, but they frequently do. In this instance, they did. So we watched the short video again.

At this point, I had to restrain myself. I wanted to explain what they were seeing in the video in more depth. I wanted to be sure they understood. Instead, I bit my tongue and trusted that our conversation would get us there. I didn't want to make the same mistake I'd made when reading *Pink and Say* (described in Chapter 3) to my students in my first year of

144

FIGURE 5.3

Student notes from a variety of third-grade conversations: The top two notes are from conversations about *Rad Women Worldwide*—the first about Qui Jin, a Chinese revolutionary in the late nineteenth century, and the second about Nanny of the Maroons, an eighteenth-century leader of formerly enslaved people in Jamaica. On the bottom left is a student note from a conversation about ICE raids in local neighborhoods. The final note is from a discussion of Blue Balliett's *Hold Fast*, a novel that explores class, race, homelessness, and interactions with police.

teaching. I didn't want to hammer a point so hard that it left little room for my students to grapple with ideas and questions themselves. So, after our second viewing, I asked students to stop and write or draw about their thinking, in whatever way made the most sense for them. I wanted to keep their responses as open-ended as possible.

As in our earlier conversation about the Emancipation Proclamation, some students grabbed a pen and quickly got going, while others continued to sit still. I remained still for a few moments as well. If I had walked around, students who were hesitant might have felt pressure to write or draw something, causing stress rather than reflection. I wanted them to feel that they had the space and time to process what they had seen. I typically do not collect these reflection drawings and thoughts, not wanting students to view these as something that will be graded or judged. Later in the year, when students know our routines and trust me, I can collect them without as much concern about impacting what they are drawing or writing. Again, I want this strategy to help students think deeply. If they see it as something I am going to collect and judge, they will feel constrained to respond in ways they think I want to see. On occasion, students have given me these pages, wanting to share their thoughts with me. But I don't require it.

> I didn't want to hammer a point so hard that it left little room for my students to grapple with ideas and questions themselves.

When we were ready to share, which I gauged based on students beginning to put down pens and look around or even engage in some side conversations, I was at another crossroad. Do I prompt this discussion with a targeted, specific question, or do I keep it open-ended and ask students to share their thinking? I was prepared with prompts, but I had to decide when to use them. When making this decision, I try to see how intently students are focused on their personal reflections on a text. If they seem all-in, I lean toward open-ended sharing. If they seem less sure, I am more likely to warm them up with a targeted question. This group was pretty evenly split between students who seemed to have a lot to say and students who were unsure. As this was an intense topic, I decided to start off with a targeted question in order to bring as many students as possible into the conversation. I asked students, "What did you find surprising about Ruby Bridges and her first-grade year?" Hands shot up in the air.

Justin looked like he might explode if he didn't get to share, so I let him get us rolling. He said, "I was really surprised that it was just her and her teacher!"

Inside, I was thrilled. This was one of the points in the video that I thought students might have missed. Based on their looks of surprise, it seemed that some of his classmates *had* missed it. Others were eagerly making the "connection sign" (thumb and pinky finger pointing out, moving their hand between their chest and Justin's direction), showing that they'd been surprised by the same thing. I asked, "Can you imagine that? If it was just you and me, all year long?" A few kids giggled at the thought. "That does seem very strange and surprising," I continued. "What do you think about that?"

Ashley, who had looked surprised by Justin's statement, said, "I don't understand. Where were Ruby Bridges's classmates?"

Justin responded immediately: "She didn't have any!"

Ashley pushed back, saying, "But why not? Everyone has classmates!" as she waved her hands around, proving her point with the existence of all of us, together in our classroom.

I waited, watching my students process that question. Even Justin, who had been so confident in his understanding of this idea, looked a bit perplexed. As I had expected this point to be a difficult one for my students (or one they didn't even notice), I knew exactly where I wanted to return in the video. I jumped to the moment in which Ruby Bridges said, "Mrs. Henry was the only teacher that would teach me." I asked, "What do you think that means?"

It was quiet for a moment. Amina hesitantly raised her hand. "Maybe the other teachers didn't like her?" She said it more as a question than a statement.

Ashley looked at Amina. "That's true. All those people yelling at her didn't like her. Maybe the teachers didn't either. They didn't like her because she was Black." I could hear in Ashley's voice a sense of betrayal at the idea that *teachers*, of all people, might have acted that way. It was something I hadn't considered and wasn't prepared to address. In hindsight, it was a big thing not to have anticipated. It shouldn't have come as a surprise that my students would struggle with the specific idea that *teachers* were racist. I made a quick note, because I didn't want one of the takeaways from this conversation to be that teachers would abandon children because of the color of their skin. It wasn't the time to address it right then, but I definitely wanted to remember it, to return to it later in the conversation or in another way very soon. In this moment, I wanted the class to follow the thread Justin and Amina had started.

> I could hear in Ashley's voice a sense of betrayal at the idea that *teachers*, of all people, might have acted that way.

I said, "Justin was surprised that it was just Ruby Bridges and her teacher, that she didn't have any classmates. What are you thinking about that idea now?"

Justin had clearly been on that track already and said, "Maybe the other kids didn't want to be in her class because she was Black. Why did people care so much about that? Who cares if you're Black?" His classmates nodded their heads.

Amina, with more confidence than before, said, "That's so wrong. They're just kids. Why would they not like her because she's Black? We all like each other!"

Nala jumped in with a big smile. "And when we don't like each other, it isn't because someone is Black!" Her classmates giggled at that while they agreed with her.

I decided that was the moment to try to bring their thinking around to how the past impacts the present (or, in this case, how the more distant past had impacted the more recent past). I reminded the students of our discussion of the Constitution and whose voices were a part of creating our laws, our government, and our country. I told them that the great-grandkids of those men were the ones who were either freeing enslaved people or fighting to keep slavery. And now, the great-grandkids of *those* people are Ruby Bridges and her possible classmates. "How might the way our country was formed have impacted what happened when Ruby Bridges started first grade?"

Such a big question warranted a lot of wait time.

148

Ashley finally broke the silence. "It feels like people didn't like Black people for a long time." She said it somewhat quietly, with a heaviness.

Tahir responded, "Yeah. A long time ago they had slaves, but even when Black people weren't slaves, they were still treated bad. It's like people acted like they were still slaves."

Justin added a thought: "They weren't acting like they were still slaves. No one made Ruby Bridges do their work. But they still didn't like her just because she was Black." Heads slowly nodded at these ideas. My students' faces still showed a mix of emotions—some confusion, some frustration, some sadness.

After a moment of quiet, as I waited to see if anyone wanted to add anything, I said, "You are starting to see how things that happened in the past can still have an impact many years later. That's a really big idea that we will continue to think about and talk about. For the moment, we'll take some deep breaths and reflect on today's discussion. I think some of you, maybe all of you, learned some surprising things today and maybe you feel a little bit different. How do you think today's conversation impacted you? . . . Maybe how it impacted you is about what you learned, or what surprised you, or what questions you have now that you weren't thinking about before." I stopped to give them a moment to think. Quickly, hands went up, but I wanted them all to have a chance to talk, so after waiting about a minute, I said, "Turn and talk to a partner about what you're thinking about."

Sometimes I want to make sure we wrap up a conversation all together. I want us to end as a whole class, like a final chord in a song, bringing closure for all of us. Other times, I want to be sure every student has a chance to talk through their own reflection. The processing that happens as students share their thinking, the way they think about it more carefully as they tell it to a peer, can help them close the conversation for themselves—in a way that might not happen if only a few students get the chance to talk.

Students eagerly turned to a partner, some of them overflowing with what they wanted to say, and others sharing more quietly. I noticed, as they shared, that many of my third graders specifically needed the chance to say out loud things that *surprised* them. There's a power to verbally stating surprising information—putting this information into words can make it feel more real.

- I'm so surprised that some people still don't like Black people. I don't get that.

- I can't imagine a classroom with just me and a teacher. That's so weird.

- Ruby Bridges is still alive! I wonder if my mom and dad know that.

My third graders definitely didn't have all of the answers by the time we wrapped up this conversation. They did, however, have lots of great questions and interest in continuing to think and learn about how the past has impacted our present. As I listened to their partner talk, I found their engagement with the topic, frankly, energizing. I knew that they were now more likely, as the year went on, to thoughtfully link new conversations about race and racism in our present to relevant issues from our past.

CHAPTER 6

VOTING RIGHTS IN UPPER ELEMENTARY

I n Chapter 3 we described the importance of *threading*, arguing that some race conversations benefit from being continued across the course of weeks, months, or even the entire school year. This prolonged engagement offers students the chance to sit longer with questions and ideas, to develop their thinking more deeply, and to continually add new perspectives and thoughts to specific racial understandings. At times, a threaded conversation can have a strong start, a big conversation that dramatically kicks off an idea. Other times, a threaded conversation might begin with small stitches, carefully placed. That is the kind of conversation we'll explore in this chapter.

In general, upper-elementary students will be able to explore more complex ideas and questions about race than their younger counterparts. They have a broader wealth of knowledge, simply from having more years of school and more lived experiences. These lived experiences are likely to include specific personal experiences or previous race conversations that have informed their feelings about the specific race topic. In addition to this, older elementary kids also have generally stronger conversation skills gained from more years of speaking with others. This all makes for different challenges in facilitating race conversations in the upper-elementary grades. Planning for these conversations requires us to thoughtfully reflect about our students' background knowledge and developmental stages, and about their sophistication with language and conversation skills.

CONNECTING TO THE STANDARDS

GRADE 5 ENGLISH STANDARDS

5.1 The student will use effective oral communication skills in a variety of settings.

  b) Participate in and contribute to discussions across content areas.

  d) Orally express ideas clearly in pairs, diverse groups, and whole-class settings.

5.3 The student will learn how media messages are constructed and for what purposes.

  b) Identify the characteristics and effectiveness of a variety of media messages.

5.6 The student will read and demonstrate comprehension of nonfiction texts.

  b) Skim materials to develop a general overview of content and to locate specific information.

  g) Locate information to support opinions, inferences, and conclusions.

5.7 The student will write in a variety of forms to include narrative, descriptive, expository, and persuasive.

  e) Organize information to convey a central idea.

(Virginia Department of Education 2017, 21–23)

WHO CAN VOTE?

Over the course of the year, my fifth-grade class worked together to create a time line of important events throughout the history of the United States. By the spring, we had a detailed time line at hand, including a number of events related to voting rights. To prepare for the conversation I was planning, I transferred events related to voting to a new time line, to make them easier to focus on. I then displayed both time lines so that students could reference other events in addition to the ones specifically

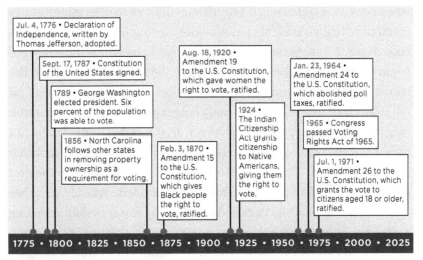

FIGURE 6.1
A time line of events in voting rights history that Jen's class
used to spark conversation

about voting. To begin, I pointed at the voting time line and asked, "What
do you notice and what do you wonder about this time line? Take a few
moments and write down your thoughts about what you see."

As we saw with the middle-elementary conversation in Chapter 5, giving
students time to write about their thoughts is a beneficial way to warm
up. It especially helps upper-elementary students for a variety of reasons:

- It gives them permission to take some time to look closely and
  think without feeling they have to speak immediately.

- It forces them to slow down and not just say the first things
  they notice.

- It allows them to order their own thoughts before hearing from
  their peers. This makes it less likely that they just follow the lead of
  whoever starts the conversation, or whoever has the strongest voice.

By this point in the school year, my students have responded to the general prompts "What do you notice?" and "What do you wonder?" multiple
times across all content areas. They are both familiar and comfortable with
responding to these questions. So I waited a few minutes, watching to see

when pens were laid down. It's sometimes difficult to determine just how much time to give students to jot before moving on. There needs to be enough time for everyone to have ideas, but not so much that these thoughts begin to wander in other directions. As students are all individuals, that moment won't be the same for all of them. Sometimes I feel confident I can tell from facial expressions and body language when to move on. Other times I need feedback from my students. In this case, I wanted to be sure they'd had enough time, so I used the "fist of five" technique described in Chapter 3. I asked, "On a fist of five, how many more minutes do you need before we talk?" Familiar with this routine, students quickly shot their hands in the air. Some had a closed fist, showing that they didn't need any more time. Enough hands, however, went up indicating two or three more minutes. So I told them to take two more minutes to write.

At the end of this time, I asked students to turn and talk with a partner about what they noticed and wondered about the voting time line. I walked around the room, listening in on conversations and keeping my eyes open for any sign of conflict.

As I roamed around the room, I heard statements like these:

- "I'm noticing it was about two hundred years before everyone had the right to vote."

- "I wonder why North Carolina was the last state to make it so all White men could vote. And what was the first state? How long did it take before all states did it?"

- "I'm noticing, *again*, that Native Americans couldn't vote for a really long time. That's so wrong."

One partnership had an especially interesting conversation. It started with D'Jori saying, "I noticed the Fifteenth Amendment gave Black people the right to vote, but about a hundred years later the Voting Rights Act was passed because they weren't *really* being able to vote."

Her partner, Gavin, turned his head to look at the time line. He responded, "Oh. Yeah. Wow. I wonder if other groups of people supposedly had the right to vote but really didn't."

D'Jori said, "Yeah, I mean, we know White men could always vote, but at first it was only the ones who owned property. It seems like everybody had times they *could* vote but couldn't *actually* vote." I made a mental note to be sure to invite D'Jori and Gavin to share with the whole class.

As I brought the whole group together, I said, "It sounds like some of you were noticing things that you had noticed before. Looking at this time line is reinforcing some ideas you already had. I definitely did some of that when I looked at it. Right now, though, let's focus on sharing things that we noticed or wondered that were *new* or surprising to us." I worded the question this way to keep our conversation focused on new ideas. Since we had created and examined this time line again and again throughout the year, I knew students had thoughts about it from previous discussions. It would have been easy for us to get back into ideas from previous lessons, and I wanted us to move forward on voting rights.

BUT CAN THEY REALLY VOTE?

A few students shared ideas, and their classmates listened closely, heads mostly nodding but sometimes cocked sideways with looks of skepticism or uncertainty. I then asked D'Jori and Gavin to share what they had noticed and wondered. Just as Gavin had immediately turned to the time line when D'Jori stated her thought, other classmates did so now. D'Jori and Gavin's observation and question about whether legally having the right to vote meant people could actually vote intrigued many of their classmates. Quickly the class seemed split between students whose hands were in the air and students whose eyes were squinting at the time line.

I debated whether to continue the whole-class conversation or to pause it for a bit to allow students to talk briefly with a partner. I opted for the partner check-in because it would allow all those students with hands waving to share their thoughts, while also giving all those kids still process-

> I prompted them with "Do you think legally having the right to vote means a person can *actually* vote? Turn and talk with a partner about that question."

ing a little more time and the chance to hear ideas from someone else. I prompted them with "Do you think legally having the right to vote means a person can *actually* vote? Turn and talk with a partner about that question."

As I walked around the room, I found that quite a few students believed that in the past, legally having the right to vote had not always meant people could actually vote, but they were certain that now it did. This belief was very strong for a number of students, and their passion for it seemed to be convincing their partners. Other students were not so sure, noting the time it took for Black Americans and Native Americans to truly be able to vote. I overheard Stephanie bring up a critical point when she said to her partner, "If the Fifteenth Amendment didn't really mean Black people had the right to vote, how can we be sure that the Voting Rights Act did?" I made a mental note to invite Stephanie to share this with the whole group, because it was such an astute question. She was likely the only student who had made this connection.

When we returned to our whole-group discussion a few minutes later, I asked Stephanie to share her question. Many of her classmates who firmly believed that nowadays everyone with the right to vote is truly *able* to vote looked a little stunned. Classmates who had been skeptical of the idea that having the *right* to vote meant that one always *could* vote looked triumphant, as if their point had been proven. Wanting to build upon Stephanie's question and the emotions it was evoking in my students, I asked them, "What impacts who can vote? We know that *laws* make a difference in who can vote, but it seems there are other factors. What else might make a difference?" My ultimate goal had been for students to wrestle with these prompts, and I was thrilled that we got to them naturally, building upon the insights they had shared!

The classroom went quiet as students considered this prompt. In an attempt to spur their thinking, as I realized my prompt likely needed to be more targeted, I added, "What kept Black people from being able to vote after the Fifteenth Amendment was ratified? What might have kept women from voting after the Nineteenth Amendment was? What might keep some people from voting *today*?" These, I hoped, would give students who were feeling lost a reminder of helpful historical context we'd covered earlier.

Elle slowly raised her hand and shared, "I think some women didn't vote back then because they didn't really think it was their place. They didn't see it as something women were supposed to do?"

As she ended her idea as if it were a question, I stepped in again. "Thank you, Elle, for getting us started. What do you all think of Elle's idea about why women might not have voted in the past? That maybe women didn't think they were supposed to vote." I hoped that both my encouragement and her classmates' reactions would allow Elle to gain some confidence.

Jordan responded, "Yeah, I think that's true, Elle. But I think it's more than that. Lots of men didn't want women to vote back then, so maybe they were afraid to."

Cullen added his thoughts: "And maybe their husbands or their dads or brothers or whoever didn't want them to vote and told them not to." Lots of heads nodded at these ideas.

I tried to bring these thoughts together: "So it sounds like you have several ideas for what kept people from voting, even when they legally had the right to do so. Maybe they felt uncomfortable with it because it wasn't something they'd seen people like themselves do before, because it was a new right. Maybe they were afraid of how other people would treat them if they voted. Or maybe people in their lives told them not to vote. Those are all really interesting ideas. Do you think those things would keep people from voting *now*?"

Rameen, a young student who was usually pretty quiet during class discussions, raised his hand and said, "I know there are people in our neighborhood who don't vote because they're afraid to." He paused, and I held my breath, hoping his classmates would give him the space to continue. Many looked at him in disbelief, and their surprise kept them quiet for a bit. He finally went on: "Some people don't have papers, so they can't vote. Some people do have papers but they're afraid of getting in trouble with the authorities or getting deported, so they don't do things like vote because it would make them get noticed."

I thanked Rameen for sharing his idea and helping us connect what we had learned about voting in the past to voting today. To wrap up the first day of this conversation, I said, "You've done some serious thinking today about who could vote throughout our country's history. And then you've thought deeply about who could *really* vote back in the past and what might have impacted that. We're going to continue this discussion tomorrow, exploring who *does* vote now and why that might be."

The kids could clearly have continued talking, but I preferred to stop the conversation before their stamina ran out. When that happens, some students get distracted, some poke at their neighbors, some stare off into space or get fidgety, and then our conversation loses focus. By the upper-elementary grades, students typically have the stamina to focus for longer periods. They are, however, still fairly young, and—especially when it comes to conversations that are challenging or emotional—keeping our conversation time on the shorter end can be beneficial.

DAY TWO: CONTINUING THE CONVERSATION

"Yesterday we did some deep thinking about who could vote throughout our country's history and what that truly meant. You asked some really important questions and made some thoughtful observations. Today we're going to take that thinking on to the present day and talk about who can vote and who *does* vote. So, who is able to vote right now?" I kicked off our second day of discussion in this way. I wanted to remind my students about all of the questions and ideas they'd discussed the day before so that those would be fresh in their minds as we moved forward.

Students immediately began throwing out ideas about who is able to vote today.

"White people!"

"Native Americans can!"

"Women are able to vote!"

"People of color can vote!"

It was clear that, due to the wording of my prompt, students were focused on thinking about who had been given the *right* to vote over the years. I needed to get them a little more focused. So I phrased it a bit differently, "Who is not able to vote right now?" That made them pause briefly.

Pretty quickly, Josue spoke up. "We can't vote." His classmates nodded their heads, some with clear frustration.

"Why not?" I asked him.

He responded, "You have to be eighteen years old to vote."

"Okay," I said. "We have one limitation on voting. You have to be eighteen years old before you are eligible to vote. What other restrictions are there or *might* there be?" That wording opened the door a little wider. Rather than just asking about the restrictions that currently exist, I asked what *might* exist. That hopefully communicated that students didn't have to know for sure in order to participate in the conversation.

Rameen brought up his point from the previous day: "People who don't have papers can't vote."

"Right," I said. "To vote you have to be a citizen of the United States. That's another limitation on voting. Any others you are thinking about?" As we mentioned in Chapter 2, it's often difficult to know exactly how much time to spend on a warm-up prompt. I wanted this "Who can't vote?" exchange to be fairly quick, because it was only meant to set up the meat of the conversation. I waited for a bit, but the students remained quiet. They were clearly thinking about it, but it seemed we had listed all they were willing to share at the moment. I wrote those two ideas, "being 18" and "being a U.S. citizen," on the board for future reference.

WHO ACTUALLY VOTES?

My next prompt was "Who do you think votes most often?" I deliberately kept the question broad and open-ended, knowing I could narrow it later. I knew that if I started off too narrow, it would be harder to move kids' focus back to a broader question. I told students that we would discuss this question with partners before taking it to a whole-class format. I encouraged them to help each other brainstorm.

I walked around the room, listening in on conversations. There was quite a bit of uncertainty. I heard "I don't really get it. What does she mean?" and "I have no idea who votes the most often. How would I know that?" This uncertainty had me immediately rethinking my decision to keep the question so open-ended. I decided to narrow the question. So I said, "We already said that if you're younger than eighteen, you can't vote. So everyone eighteen and older can. Do you think people in certain times of their lives are more likely or less likely to vote? Maybe men vote more often than women, or the other way around. How about by race or religion or language spoken at home? Do you think any of those things impacts how many people vote? Talk with your partner." This got conversations going.

Students were willing to discuss and debate possibilities with their partners now that they knew that none of them had the only "right" answer for this prompt. Most of their thoughts came, not surprisingly, from their own experiences. I heard comments like "My mom always votes but my dad doesn't, so I think more women vote than men," and "I think my parents vote, but I know my big brother doesn't, and he's old enough to." Students were reflecting on who they observed voting and what that might mean for larger trends.

Samantha noted, "When I go with my parents to vote, the people who are working there are all really old. Maybe old people vote more."

Kennedy and Jordan debated about the impact of history on voting. Kennedy suggested that, because White people had always been able to vote, maybe they wouldn't really think about it so much, and people who hadn't always been able to vote would be more likely to care about it. Jordan disagreed. He thought people who had always had the right to vote would do it no matter what. Other people might not be as confident as voters. He said, "Like we talked about, maybe some people don't think they're really supposed to vote, or other people tell them not to."

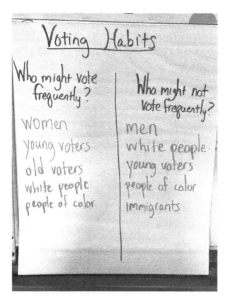

FIGURE 6.2
"Voting Habits" chart created by a fifth-grade class

When we returned to our whole-group discussion, I charted their thoughts about who might vote frequently and who would be less likely to do so. Because the class had conflicting ideas, many of our groups (women and men, older and younger people, etc.) ended up on both sides of our chart.

I pointed this out to students and told them I thought that was really exciting, because now we were going to look at some data. As we explained in Chapter 3, it's important for students to test theories against data that are both relevant and accessible. In this conversation, we would examine recent trends in voting. However, before digging into these data, I explained that voting trends could be complicated because there were two different kinds of numbers that might be used. They might see numbers or percentages of *eligible* voters, people who could *legally* vote. They might also see numbers or percentages of people who actually *did* vote. I told them that in elections in the United States, there are frequently a good number of eligible voters who do not vote.

In small groups, of about three students, I gave them different graphs to explore. Each of the graphs showed voter turnout in either one or several presidential elections. Depending on the graph, the turnout rates were broken out by gender, age, race, and/or education. Students were asked to analyze their graph, draw some conclusions, and be prepared to share them with the rest of the class. Some of the graphs were slightly more complicated, while others were simpler and more straightforward. I tried to distribute graphs so that each student would be able to analyze the one they received. I also had multiple copies so that all the students in a group weren't trying to huddle around one 8½" x 11" piece of paper.

After a few minutes (students didn't need too long to dig into one graph), I asked groups to share

FIGURE 6.3
Different graphs on voter participation analyzed by students in small groups

what they had learned from their discussion. Groups reported the following information:

- Women voted more than men in recent elections.

- Older people voted more than younger people.

- People who went to college voted more than people who didn't.

- People who didn't finish high school voted the least often.

- In general, White people voted the most, followed by Black people, and then Latinx people and all others.

- In 2008 and 2012, Black people voted the most.

- Some people who were eligible to vote were not registered to vote.

- The graphs jumped up and down again and again. (Why was that happening?)

I reminded them that we had federal elections every two years, for Congress, but only elect a president every four years. Voter turnout is higher in presidential election years than in other years. (This information wasn't hugely pertinent to our conversation, which is why I quickly explained these data instead of trying to guide students to understanding them through inquiry. It had been causing confusion, and a longer conversation could have distracted students from the more relevant ideas we were discussing.) One group did note that only about 70 percent of eligible voters were actually registered, and only about 60 to 65 percent of eligible voters actually voted in presidential election years.

Once we had solved the mystery of voting numbers jumping up for presidential elections and back down during midterm elections, I asked students why they thought 2008 and 2016 were different for White and Black voters than all other recent elections. As these students hadn't been born in 2008 and were quite young in 2016, this wasn't immediately obvious to them. They offered some ideas about why White people might not have taken the time to vote in those years or why Black people might have felt more confident or interested, but with some uncertainty. Then Jordan asked, "Who was running for president in those elections? Was that when Obama was elected?" And light bulbs went on around the room. The understanding was so clear and so strong, students were saying, "Oh yeah!" and "Of course!" and "That's what was going on!"

WHAT IMPACTS WHO VOTES?

I took that epiphany as an opportunity to build to my next question. "It seems like you noticed that when a Black man was running for president, that impacted who was voting in that election. Look at these other observations your classmates have made about who votes and how often they vote. Why do you think the data look this way?" My "do you think" phrasing was meant to make space for incomplete, developing theories about the data.

At this point, students had held their focus as a whole group for a while, so I opted to pivot students back to small groups. I did, however, mix up these small groups so that students weren't talking with the same classmates with whom they had been discussing the graphs. I also offered each group copies of all the graphs so that they could turn to them for reference if they wished.

As I walked around the room, listening in on various groups' conversations and answering students' questions (mostly with questions of my own), I heard a lot of theories based on the data and their observations. Students were also referring back to thoughts that had been shared earlier in the conversation. One group started off focused on age. They discussed their surprise that young people voted the least often. Their surprise stemmed from their own eagerness to be able to vote, and they couldn't imagine why others wouldn't do so as soon as they were able to.

- "Maybe old people vote most often because they're probably retired and don't really have anything else to do."

- "Why are the youngest people so low on this graph? Why wouldn't they vote?"

- "That's a big difference between the lowest votes and the highest!" (They meant the youngest and the oldest.)

Another group focused, at least for a bit, on gender. The girls in the group had a bit of a superior attitude because of those statistics. The boy was flummoxed.

- "Why don't men vote as often as women?"

- "It's not really that different. Sixty-eight percent and sixty-five percent are pretty close to the same."

- "Some moms are at home while dads are at work. It could be easier for the moms to vote."

Several groups talked about how data about race fit what they knew about American history. They theorized that since White people had been able to vote for a long time, they felt more comfortable voting. They also suggested that people of color had not been able to vote for as long, so maybe it still felt kind of weird to some. Some groups did follow up on Rameen's thoughts about whether knowing people who are in this country without papers impacted voting. They thought that some eligible voters might still be afraid to vote because they feared bringing attention to themselves or to members of their family.

It was interesting to hear some groups compare the data about race to the data about gender. White people, who could vote from the beginning (at least some of them), vote in higher numbers than others. But men, who could also vote from the beginning (at least some of them), don't vote in higher numbers than women. This was surprising to several groups.

> If students had not gotten to ideas about what keeps people from voting, I wanted to be sure they had the question at the front of their minds.

When the small groups seemed to slow down in their discussions a bit, I added to the prompt. I asked, "What do you think keeps people from voting today?" Some groups were naturally getting at that question in their conversations, but I wanted to be sure it was explicitly asked rather than implied. If students had not gotten to ideas about what keeps people from voting, I wanted to be sure they had the question at the front of their minds. My goal was to wrap up today's conversation by generating a list of their responses to this question.

By the time the small groups were ready to share, they had these thoughts ready:

- People might not vote because they don't have time.

- People might not vote because they don't feel safe doing so.

- People might not vote because they don't feel comfortable with it (they don't see it as something people like them really do).

- People might not vote because they don't think their vote matters.

- People might not vote because it can be a hassle.

The wording "People might not vote because" came from the first group's sharing and was adopted by future groups, a piece of active listening that impressed me. I was even more impressed by my students' inquiry, and I told them so. "You shared your ideas about why 'people might not vote' and did so in a way that shows you are making a hypothesis about this. That sets us up nicely for tomorrow. We are going to look at some articles about voting in the United States and see if we can confirm whether any of our theories are correct."

I had thought this whole conversation might last two days, but their group discussions had been so engaging that I had not wanted to stop students any earlier. I opted to extend our discussion to a third day rather than rein students in or cut part of my plan (both of which I have had to do in other circumstances, due to timing).

DAY THREE: CONSOLIDATING OUR IDEAS

To bring together all of the ideas from the past couple of days—thoughts on who could vote historically and when; who did/does vote and why; and what limitations there are on voting, legal or otherwise—I chose a few articles from Newsela to give students a little more information and guide the rest of our conversation. I considered having students do a jigsaw reading of the articles but decided I wanted everyone to read at least a couple of them. We started off with "Registering to Vote in U.S. Elections" (Newsela 2018). This article explains what it means to register to vote, how to go about doing so, and how that process varies from state to state. I gave each student a copy and some options.

"You can read the article independently, or you can read with a partner or in a small group. As you read, please make notes in the margins or on the back about any questions you have. You can also circle things in the article and use our shorthand to notate ["!" for surprising information, "?" for questions, etc.] if you'd like. Just make sure that you will be able to read your notes and remember what you were thinking for our discussion in a bit. You might also opt to read the article more than once and see what else you notice or wonder," I told them. Some students preferred to work independently and not be distracted in their reading. Others, because their reading skills were still developing or because they worked better in discussion with another student, preferred to work with a partner.

As the article was fairly short and we had more reading to do, I gave them just a few minutes to read, notate, and talk with a partner if they wished. Then I started off with a broad warm-up prompt: "What are you thinking now that you've read that?" I did have certain ideas that I wanted students to consider, but as in the earlier conversations, I knew that I could narrow the scope if we didn't get there naturally from a broader start. It's often worth it to see if the conversation can be sparked by a student comment, so that students can feel more ownership of the thread.

Elle raised her hand and said, "I didn't know that you can't vote if you were convicted of a crime."

From walking around, I had noticed a lot of students had made notations by that bit of information, so I wasn't surprised to find many nodding heads and some murmured agreements. "It looks like you weren't alone in that, Elle," I said. "Should we add that to our list of limitations on voting?" I saw agreement around the room, so I walked over and wrote "Not convicted of a crime" on our list, under "Age 18 or older" and "Citizen of the U.S." I then asked, "What else?"

Josue spoke up. "It seems weird that you can't vote until you're eighteen but you can register at sixteen or seventeen or something." Again, his classmates were on the same track with him.

"Yeah, and why is it different in different states? Shouldn't everyone have the same voting rules?" asked Jordan. Looking around, I could see that lots of students had thought about Josue's question but not Jordan's. I could see them processing this idea.

"Josue and Jordan bring up an interesting point," I said. "In different states you can register at different ages, although you can't vote until you're eighteen no matter what state you're in. You also can register in different ways and at different places in different states. That can make a difference in the voting trends we've been looking at. Let's take a quick look at another article that I think will give you a clearer picture on this."

I handed them "How Voting in the U.S. is Harder Than Just Checking a Box" (Newsela 2020). "As you read this article, just like before, notate, talk with a partner, think about what you notice and what you wonder, reread. But also, think about how different rules might make voting harder for different people. That's what we'll focus on when we talk in a few minutes."

As students read and notated, I saw a lot of writing. Students turned to neighbors to share something they'd read, often with surprise or outrage. I noticed that sometimes they shared information that confirmed something they'd thought or something we'd previously discussed. The article definitely had their attention. When I brought them back to the whole group, I didn't have to say anything to get them started; hands were in the air immediately.

"We do so many things online. Why shouldn't people be able to vote online?"

"We vote on Tuesdays? That seems really random. Why Tuesday?"

"So the Constitution gives states the right to decide how voting works? Weird."

"People don't vote because they're busy or because they don't like the candidates. We talked about those possibilities yesterday."

I gave students a few minutes to informally share. Then I said, "You all have a lot of thoughts from reading this article, and I can see a lot of notations on your papers. That's really exciting. Let's pause for just a moment and think back to the question I gave you before you read. Notice the title of the article. What did you learn that might make voting harder for people? Take just a moment to think and maybe look back at your notes before we start talking." I picked up my copy of the article and looked at it again, modeling for my students what I wanted them to do. I waited for a minute or so, making sure students had time to organize their thoughts. I then asked, "Where should we start? What is one thing that might be making it harder for people to vote?"

Ashley jumped back in with what she had mentioned before: "Voting happens on *Tuesdays*. That might be hard for some people."

"What do you all think? Does election day being a Tuesday make it harder for people to vote? Does it make it harder for *everyone*? Or will some people have more difficulties with the day than others?" I was focusing students on Ashley's idea, nudging her language slightly in order to make it into a prompt. This, remember, had been my goal, to get things formally started with a student idea. Every time we do this, we help students see their peers (and hopefully themselves) as knowledgeable contributors. It also sets them and their peers up as valuable teachers to one another. This prompt encouraged Ashley's classmates to think about the fairness of Tuesday voting.

Students shared some thoughts about how people's work schedules might make it hard to vote on a Tuesday. Jordan noted that his mom's work schedule wasn't always the same, so it might be hard for her to plan on voting. I also asked them if commutes or transportation could impact voter participation as well, and students were able to think through how having a long commute or not having a car and relying on public transportation could make voting more of a challenge. Elle said that her mom took the bus to work and that sometimes she had to leave extra early or get home later because of the bus schedule. Some students pointed out that the article said many states allow for early voting, which could make a difference for voters, including the parents mentioned.

Gavin said, "People have to have an ID to vote in most places. It sounds like that can make it harder."

I paused to see if any of his classmates wanted to jump in, but when they didn't, I said, "Thanks, Gavin. Why would needing to have a photo ID make it harder to vote?"

Several students connected with Gavin's uncertainty and shared thoughts about how they thought all adults had IDs. I pointed out that it had to be a photo ID, not just any ID, and that it had to be an approved one. This seemed to add to the confusion, at least for some students. "What does that mean, an approved photo ID?" asked Rameen.

Again, I waited to see if a student wanted to respond. It's always a bonus if factual information like this can come from the students. We do have to be careful, however, to not let our desire for inquiry distract us from the meat of the discussion. Since no one spoke up, I went ahead and answered so we could keep moving. "Typically that means a photo ID that is issued by the state. IDs for work or school would not be accepted. So people would have to go, typically, to the Department of Motor Vehicles and pay to get an official ID. Here in Virginia, it costs about forty-two dollars to get a driver's license, just to give you an idea of what that looks like."

"Oh," said Rameen, "so that's why the article said people with less money might not have one. You have to *pay* for it."

Ashley added on. "And you have to get to the DMV. My dad had to get a new license recently and he complained a lot about how hard it was to get there. He said it's always busy and so it can take forever to get things done. That could also make it hard for people to get an ID."

I was impressed with these observations—enough to show me that it was time to bring the threads of this three-day-long conversation together. I said, "You've noticed that *when* people can vote might impact whether or not they do. You've also noted that *what they need* in order to vote might impact whether or not they vote. Now let's think about that, but also about the data we looked at yesterday. Can these challenges to voting explain why some groups vote more often than other groups?" I sent them back to small groups.

Students immediately turned to others near them and began sharing thoughts and asking each other questions. The buzz in the room was a sign of their engagement and their confidence in this discussion. Students were looking back at their articles, referring to their graphs, and making notes as they talked. I moved about, hovering on the edge of conversations and listening in. I couldn't catch everything as students talked with partners or in small groups, but

> Students were looking back at their articles, referring to their graphs, and making notes as they talked. I moved about, hovering on the edge of conversations and listening in.

I wanted to hear any nuggets worth bringing to the whole group, or any confusion or misconceptions that I could help address.

Here are some of the thoughts they shared in their groups:

- "I still don't get why young people don't vote that much. It doesn't seem like when they can vote or needing an ID would be a big problem for young people more than for old people."

- "Maybe the ID thing is a problem for some people who weren't born in the U.S. Even if they have papers, maybe they don't have an official ID. That might be why White people vote more."

- "I think more women don't have jobs than men. Maybe that means they can vote on Tuesdays easily."

- "People who went to college probably make more money. That means they can get an ID. That makes it easier for them to vote."

- "The article also said some people don't vote because they don't like the candidates. Most of the people who run for president and stuff are White people. Maybe Black people and other people don't feel like those candidates are going to help them."

When I brought students back to the whole group, I wanted to be sure we started to consolidate all of the thinking we'd been doing over the past few days. I was concerned we would miss some ideas because we had engaged a lot of information. In order to center our "final" thoughts on data, I decided to focus on our graphs. I started with one about voting percentages by gender and asked students what they thought might be behind those numbers.

The idea of more women being home or having flexible schedules came up, and students seemed to be in agreement with that idea. I said, "As we've talked over the past few days, some of you thought women might vote less often because they haven't had the right to vote for as long as men, and that seemed to make a lot of sense to me. But *then* we found out that women vote *more* often. Now you're noticing that the scheduling of elections might be one factor. Is there anything else you think might make more women vote than men?"

After a bit of silence, while students pondered that question, D'Jori raised her hand. "The article said that some people don't vote because they don't care about the issues. Maybe women care more about the issues than men do." She didn't sound certain, and her classmates hesitantly nodded their heads, as if they weren't sure either.

I responded, "It sounds like you have a theory, D'Jori, but you don't have the data or information to be sure. That would be interesting to look into some more. Thanks for sharing your thoughts."

Next I shared the graph of voting percentages by age and asked the same question. Jordan had one thought: "Maybe people who are younger don't make as much money and so it's harder for them to get an ID than for people who are older."

"I don't know," responded Gavin. "It doesn't seem like there would be enough of a difference to make such a big difference in how many people vote. I mean, that's a lot more people voting in the next age group even. A lot! I don't think forty-two dollars would make that big a difference. I don't get it."

Others spoke up, supporting Jordan or agreeing with Gavin. Students seemed a bit perplexed, still, by how few young people vote. That was okay. This was one of many voting patterns that perplexes adults!

Next I put up voter turnout rates by race and ethnicity, and we repeated the previous process. This graph brought out more ideas which were shared with more confidence. Rameen shared his thoughts about how people who weren't born here, like many in his neighborhood, might not have official IDs and so wouldn't vote. Ashley, building on her partner conversation, shared, "D'Jori was thinking earlier about how much people care about the issues. The article also said that some people don't vote because they don't like the candidates. If most of the candidates are White, maybe people who aren't White don't feel like voting for them."

A few students immediately responded to Ashley with surprise. "Why would that make people not vote? Isn't that racist, to not vote because of the race of the people running? That seems really wrong." Ashley's face fell as she listened to some of her classmates.

When describing the previous chapter's middle-grades discussion, I mentioned a similarly tough "Should I step in?" decision during a moment of potential conflict. In that moment, trusting the kids, our relationship-building process, and my read of the moment, I'd decided to *not* immediately step in. Here, however, my read of both Ashley's and her classmates' emotional reactions and my impression that students would benefit from my reframing made me decide to step in. I said, "Ashley brings up a really important point. Most of the people who are running for office and even more of the people who have been elected are White. They may not understand what it means to be Black or Latinx or Asian or Native in our country today. People in those communities may not believe that White people will make decisions that will help them or their communities. They may not see a candidate who will work for them. We've talked before about how important it is to have books in our classroom library that are windows and mirrors for all kids. Can you think about that in a way that might be important in why people do or don't vote?"

A NOTE ABOUT CLASSROOM LIBRARIES

At the start of the school year, the students and I work together to create our classroom library. Each day, we open a box of books and explore them. After a few boxes have been opened, we begin to sort the books we have so far, while still adding books each day. Students create classroom library baskets sorted by an author, a series, or an idea (books about sea animals, books about friendship, adventure books, books about the solar system). After we sort for a few days, I begin asking questions about the books they're finding. I ask, "Are you finding books with main characters who are people of color?" or "Have you seen any books written or illustrated by people of color?" As we notice trends in our classroom library, I ask, "Can you find a book that you connect with? One with a main character that you feel similar to?" This begins our conversations around mirrors. As we look at the books each student has brought to the conversation, we talk about which books might be windows for us. Discussing Dr. Rudine Sims

Bishop's work around mirrors and windows (1990) continues throughout the year. When I conference with students about their choice reading, I might ask them if the book is a window or mirror (and it might not really be either, which is fine too). It's a conversation that is threaded throughout the year and that comes back as we discuss voting.

As students reflected on the graphs in front of them, this idea about windows and mirrors set them off and running. Again, they had thoughts:

- "That makes sense. Ashley is saying that the people we can vote for only look like some of us. They [most candidates] look like the people who vote the most. Yeah."

- "And that might explain why young people don't vote as often. Most of the people who run are older. I hadn't thought about that."

- "But what about women? We've never had a woman president. Women aren't seeing other women that much. Why do they vote so much?"

There was so much more we could have done with these conversations. We could have dug deeper with articles about the Voting Rights Act, governors restoring voting rights to those convicted of crimes, cities granting voting rights to non-citizens, and more. I was elated that my students were wrestling with the same issues that adults wrestle with, and learning how to engage them thoughtfully. This series of inquiry-driven voting conversations had turned

> I have to regularly remind myself that there is always *more* we can do and that, hopefully, students will continue to explore these ideas throughout the year, in future years, and as adults.

out exactly as I had hoped, with students asking questions about things they might previously have taken for granted, and making meaningful connections between historical events and their lives today. I have to regularly remind myself that there is always *more* we can do and that, hopefully, students will continue to explore these ideas throughout the year, in future years, and as adults. Though ending this conversation was personally hard for me—as the issue of voting rights is a passion of mine—I found comfort in the idea that these specific voting rights conversations had planted a seed that would be hard to displace.

GIANTS

A QUICK NOTE FROM A HIGH SCHOOL EDUCATOR

It's important for us teachers to remind ourselves that just because an *idea*, a *classroom practice*, or a *platitude* has become popular—or even clichéd—doesn't mean that it is wrong, lacks usefulness, or should be met with rolled eyes. For instance, this book (and *Not Light* before it) has been grounded in a fundamentally simple, and now oft-cited (especially post-2020) *idea*: students benefit from meaningful classroom race conversations. The *classroom practices* that Jen has described so thoroughly (and with so much vulnerability), are rooted in frequently cited research on inquiry and dialogic pedagogy that goes back decades—if not further. This brings me to the *platitude*—that we teachers stand on the shoulders of giants. We have all heard it. And yet, it has never been truer.

As I mentioned in the introduction to this book, I am a high school teacher who is the proud son of an exemplary career elementary school teacher. My wife, Cait, is a high school teacher who is the proud daughter of a brilliant career Montessori educator. Some of our earliest teaching experiences were in their classrooms, and we both decided to commit our lives to the care and education of young people because our mothers showed us just how meaningful a life it could be. Crucially, however, both of us realize that it's much bigger than family. Any reflection on the greatest successes we have had in our secondary classrooms will reveal that most happened in no small part because of the hard, thoughtful work of educators like Jen. They—*you*—are our giants.

Secondary educators are able to dream big, design ambitiously, and teach tough stuff with confidence because elementary teachers have set solid foundations for our students. This typically means foundations in reading and mathematical fluency, writing ability, and general knowledge about social studies. And yes, thank you for that. But just as much, we appreciate the *habits of discourse* and *epistemological stances* that you, like Jen, introduce, model, practice, and assess. While you might not see all of the fruits of your labor in the time you work with your kids, we surely see them in the years that follow. Conversations with your alumni reveal so much that one might assume they'd forgotten and, to be frank, also reveal gaps between *your* students and those not fortunate enough to have had enough teachers whose pedagogy included meaningful race conversations.

> Secondary educators are able to dream big, design ambitiously, and teach tough stuff with confidence because elementary teachers have set solid foundations for our students.

Here, for instance, are some of the benefits we reap:

1. **When you teach students that *their* lived experiences are not the *only* lived experiences** . . . secondary teachers can more easily help students who come from different K–8 schools to build rich, layered, and lasting relationships with each other.

2. **When you teach students that, while their opinions are important and worthy of respect, they are not automatically the *only* valid opinions on any given issue, and that *evidence* should be the deciding factor when opinions conflict** . . . secondary teachers can more easily lead classroom discussions (and, yes, sometimes debates) about race that, while passionate, don't immediately descend into unproductive fights.

3. **When you teach students that historical icons, politicians, celebrities, and authors were/are *people*, not infallible gods** . . . secondary *students* can more richly (a) discuss the good, the bad, and the ugly of the Founding Fathers and the systems they created, (b) investigate contemporary politicians and the policies that influence their lives, and (c) analyze texts incisively without being encumbered

by hero worship (or the assumption that their teacher expects hero worship!).

4. **When you teach students that it is not a weakness to change their minds when confronted with better information** . . . secondary teachers will be able to incorporate structures meant to offer students feedback on their ideas, and this feedback—from peers, teachers, family, and mentors— is more likely to be honestly engaged with, evaluated, and, if it makes sense, followed.

5. **When you encourage students to authentically appreciate and openly celebrate the beauty of cultural differences** . . . secondary teachers will be excited to expose these young people to even more cool stuff from different cultures, with the general understanding that these ideas, concepts, and stories will be appreciated.

And there is so much more that your hard work helps us accomplish! All to say, in case we secondary teachers don't say it enough, *thank you*. And also, know that your commitment to the discussion strategies described in this book will pay enormous dividends not only in the latter half of your students' formal education but in their future relationships, careers, and lives as thoughtful, passionate members of our society.

PROFESSIONAL REFERENCES

Allyn, Pam. 2021. "Creating Community by Reading Aloud." *Language Magazine*, January 12. https://www.languagemagazine.com /2021/01/12/creating -community-by-reading-aloud/.

Banse, Holland, Timothy W. Curby, Natalia A. Palacios, and Sara E. Rimm-Kaufman. 2018. "How Should Fifth-Grade Mathematics Teachers Start the School Year? Relations between Teacher-Student Interactions and Mathematics Instruction over One Year." *Teachers College Record* 120 (6): 1–36.

Birnbaum, Jordan. 2018. "What a Load of . . . Cognition! The Crucial Importance of Cognitive Load in Training." Training Industry, November 7. https://trainingindustry.com /articles/content-development /what-a-load-of-cognition -the-crucial-importance-of -cognitive-load-in-training/.

Bishop, Rudine Sims. 1990. "Mirrors, Windows, and Sliding Glass Doors." *Perspectives: Choosing and Using Books for the Classroom* 6(3):ix–xi.

Boaler, Jo. 2022. *Mathematical Mindsets: Unleashing Students' Potential through Creative Mathematics, Inspiring Messages and Innovative Teaching.* Hoboken, NJ: Jossey-Bass.

Burrell, Teal. 2018. "The Science Behind Interrupting: Gender, Nationality and Power, and the Roles They Play." *Post Magazine*, March 14. https://www.scmp.com /magazines/post-magazine /long-reads/article/2137023 /science-behind-interrupting -gender-nationality.

Calfee, Robert C., and Roxanne Greitz Miller. 2007. "Best Writing Practices in Assessment." In *Best Practices in Writing Instruction*, ed. Steve Graham, Charles A. MacArthur, and Michael A. Hebert. New York: Guilford Press.

Dewar, Gwen. 2019. "Working Memory in Children: What Parents and Teachers Need to Know." *Parenting Science*. https://parentingscience.com /working-memory/.

Douglass, Frederick. 1852. "What to the Slave Is the Fourth of July?" Oration to Rochester Ladies' Anti-Slavery Association. Rochester, NY. July 5.

Jacobson, Danielle, and Nida Mustafa. 2019. "Social Identity Map: A Reflexivity Tool for Practicing Explicit Positionality in Critical Qualitative Research." *International Journal of Qualitative Methods* 18:1–12. https://journals.sagepub .com/doi/pdf/10.1177 /1609406919870075.

Kahneman, Daniel. 2011. *Thinking, Fast and Slow.* New York: Farrar, Straus and Giroux.

Kay, Matthew R. 2018. *Not Light, But Fire: How to Lead Meaningful Race Conversations in the Classroom.* Portsmouth, NH: Stenhouse.

History Channel. 2014. "American Freedom Stories: Children's Crusade of 1963." YouTube video, 4:12. https://www. youtube.com /watch?v=WV0k-3Hkjsw.

Kleinrock, Liz. 2021. *Start Here, Start Now: A Guide to Antibias and Antiracist Work in Your School Community.* Portsmouth, NH: Heinemann.

National Endowment for the Humanities. *Picturing America.* National Endowment for the Humanities. https:// www.neh.gov/explore /picturing-america.

Perry, Imani. 2021. "To You: A Vulnerable Mother, A Choreo-Essay." In *You Are Your Best Thing: Vulnerability, Shame Resilience, and the Black Experience*, ed. Tarana Burke and Brené Brown. New York: Random House.

Responsive Classroom. 2016. "What Is a Morning Meeting?."https://www .responsiveclassroom.org /what-is-morning-meeting/.

Stern, Julie. 2019. "What Is Schema? How Do We Help Students Build It?" *EducationWeek*, October 20. https://www.edweek.org /education/opinion-what-is -schema-how-do-we-help -students-build-it/2019/10.

US Department of Education. 2005. "Notice of Implementation of Constitution Day and Citizenship Day on September 17 of Each Year." *Federal Register: The Daily Journal of the United States Government.* https://www .federalregister.gov /documents/2005/05/24/05 -10355/notice-of-implementation -of-constitution-day-and -citizenship-day-on-september -17-of-each-year.

Vasquez, Vivian. 2014. *Negotiating Critical Literacies with Young Children.* 2nd ed. New York: Routledge.

Virginia Department of Education. 2015. "History and Social Science Standards of Learning for Virginia Public Schools." Virginia Department of Education. https://www .doe.virginia.gov/testing /sol/standards_docs /history_socialscience/.

Virginia Department of Education. 2017. "English Standards of Learning for Virginia Public Schools." Virginia Department of Education. https://doe .virginia.gov/testing/sol /standards_docs/english /2017/stds-all-english-2017 .docxhttps://doe.virginia.gov /testing/sol/standards_docs /english/2017/stds-all -english-2017.docx.

White, Taneasha. 2021. "How Intent and Impact Differ and Why It Matters." *Healthline*, April 27. https://www .healthline.com/health /intent-vs-impact.

CHILDREN'S BOOK REFERENCES AND OTHER RESOURCES FOR CHILDREN

Byers, Grace. 2018. *I Am Enough*. Illustrated by Keturah A. Bobo. New York: Balzer + Bray.

Cherry, Matthew A. 2019. *Hair Love*. Illustrated by Vashti Harrison. New York: Kokila.

De la Peña, Matt. 2015. *Last Stop on Market Street*. Illustrated by Christian Robinson. New York: G. P. Putnam's Sons.

Harris, Mia L. 2019. *Black Girl Magic*. Illustrated by Tiffany Wilson. Self-published, Basik Studios.

Kates, Bobbi. 1992. *We're Different, We're the Same*. Illustrated by Joe Mathieu. New York: Random House.

Khan, Rukhsana. 2010. *Big Red Lollipop*. Illustrated by Sophie Blackall. New York: Viking Books for Young Readers.

Martinez-Neal, Juana. 2018. *Alma and How She Got Her Name*. Somerville, MA: Candlewick.

Newsela. 2020. "How Voting in the U.S. Is Harder Than Just Checking a Box." Newsela, May 28. https://newsela.com/read /lib-how-voting-in-US-is-hard /id/2001009207/.

Newsela. 2018. "Registering to Vote in U.S. Elections." Newsela, October 30. https://newsela.com /read/lib-register-to-vote /id/47136/.

O'Neill Grace, Catherine, and Margaret M. Bruchac. 2004. *1621: A New Look at Thanksgiving*. New York: National Geographic Kids.

Polacco, Patricia. 1994. *Pink and Say*. New York: Philomel Books.

Reynolds, Jason, and Ibram X. Kendi. 2020. *Stamped: Racism, Antiracism, and You*. New York: Little Brown.

Roe, Mechal Renee. 2021. *Cool Cuts*. New York: Doubleday Books for Young Readers.

Rotner, Shelley, and Sheila M. Kelly. 2010. *Shades of People*. New York: Holiday House.

Scholastic. 2021. "Celebrating Ruby Bridges." YouTube video, 3:51. https://www.youtube.com /watch?v=dkMDD2L70Sg.

Stone, Nic. 2018. *Dear Martin*. New York: Ember.

Thaler, Mike. 2008. *The Teacher from the Black Lagoon*. Illustrated by Jared Lee. New York: Cartwheel Books.

Thomas, Angie. 2022. *The Hate U Give*. New York: Balzer + Bray.

Thompkins-Bigelow, Jamilah. 2020. *Your Name Is a Song*. Illustrated by Luisa Uribe. New York: Innovation Press.

Tocco, Nicole. 2020. "A Color for Everyone." *Scholastic News*, August 31. https://sn4 .scholastic.com/issues/2020 -21/083120/a-color-for-everyone .html#On%20Level.

Wallace, Sandra Neil. 2018. *Between the Lines: How Ernie Barnes Went from the Football Field to the Art Gallery*. Illustrated by Bryan Collier. New York: Simon & Schuster.

Wiles, Deborah. 2005. *Freedom Summer*. Illustrated by Jerome Lagarrigue. New York: Aladdin Paperbacks.

Woodson, Jacqueline. 2018. *The Day You Begin*. Illustrated by Rafael López. New York: Nancy Paulsen Books.

Woodson, Jacqueline. 2012. *Each Kindness*. Illustrated by E. B. Lewis. New York: Nancy Paulsen Books.

INDEX

f = figure

Printed in the USA
CPSIA information can be obtained
at www.ICGtesting.com
LVHW012356181123
764224LV00078B/3434